RVICE

e the

L.32/

UH-1 IROQUOIS/ AH-1 HUEYCOBRA

Modern Combat Aircraft 19

UH-1 IROQUOIS/
AH-1 HUEYCOBRA

Jerry Scutts

LONDON

IAN ALLAN LTD

Front cover:
**A US Army AH-1S HueyCobra of Bravo Company, 501st
Aviation Battalion based at Ansbach, FRG.**
Ben J. Ullings

First published 1984

ISBN 0 7110 1416 7

Published by Ian Allan Ltd, Shepperton, Surrey;
and printed by Ian Allan Printing Ltd at their works
at Coombelands in Runnymede, England.

Contents

Introduction

Doubtless there will be fuller accounts than this one of the career of the Huey; I regard it as little more than a primer to a vast story. But maybe it will interest those who, like the author at one time, regarded the praise of the merits of helicopters in general as a little trite. Some years ago though I came to appreciate what the Huey represented, liked the look of it and found a desire to find out something of its development and combat career. At the end of writing this book I was a staunch 'Huey lover', and hopefully it will win some more converts for this remarkable helicopter.

Jerry Scutts
London

Aviation history is liberally sprinkled with aircraft that have advanced their particular 'state of the art' by a significant degree; not all of them were necessarily the first of their kind, or even the best. The Bell UH-1 is certainly not the first successful military helicopter of the postwar period, but is surely the *most* successful. And the best? That question begs some comparison with other types, but for years the Huey was the only helicopter in its class. And you don't, as Bell has, get to build more than 26,600 examples of a product that is below par.

The UH-1 was not only the first of the US Army's turbine-powered helicopters, it revolutionised that service's fundamental thinking on the support of ground troops in the field; it was for years the one helicopter that got them there and back, brought medical aid to them when they were wounded — and gave them devastatingly effective fire support during their operations. Development of the UH-1 gunship helicopters was in itself an innovation — one that was to lead to one even more significant in the shape of the first attack helicopter, the AH-1G HueyCobra. Both these Bell helicopters changed the US Army out of all recognition, winning for it along the way an independence undreamed of in the 'pre-Huey' period.

There are few corners of the world today that are not familiar with Bell UH-1s, built either by the parent firm in Texas, or in Italy, Germany, Japan or China. Proved beyond any doubt in the long, bitter debacle of Vietnam, carried to sea in ships and having traversed countless millions of miles of desert, tundra, jungle, prairie and urban conurbation, the UH-1 and its derivatives will be remembered long after the last one's rotor blades have turned for the final time. And that time is many years away.

Acknowledgements

Once again friends and colleagues have rallied to my pleas for information for a book, mainly on the all-important photographic side. Thanks are extended to them all including: Bruce Robertson; Mike Hooks; Roger Warren; Eric Allen; Gregory Alegi; Peter Newark; Rudi Pack; the staff of the Civil Aviation Authority Library; RAF Germany; the US Army, Air Force, Navy and Marine Corps; the Italian Defence Ministry; Barbra Knizner, Washington Chapter of IPMS; the photographic staff of *Soldier* magazine; R. L. Tring of the Museum of Army Flying; Oerlikon-Buhrle AG; the US Customs; and Boeing-Vertol.

Special thanks are due to Barry Wheeler, George Pennick, Dick Ward and Ray Bonds, and to *Flight International* for permission to quote from part of an interview with an Israeli Air Force officer concerning the AH-1S.

Due acknowledgement is also made to the writings of Lou Drendel and Bob Chenoweth, both leaders in the field of UH-1 operations and markings. Also invaluable in preparing this book has been Shelby L. Stanton's massive *Vietnam Order of Battle*, a major work on US Army operations in SE Asia.

All possible thanks are also extended to Marty Reisch, head of the News Bureau of Bell Helicopter Textron, who supplied many of the photographs and much useful data. Last but in no way least is Pete Harlem of the Cobra Company, an organisation dedicated to documenting US helicopter operations. Pete's help in clarifying a few 'grey areas' at very short notice is greatly appreciated.

1.
A New Kind of Army

to establish an airborne army centred round an air-mobile division. A helicopter company of H-19s and H-34s was made available for field trials and a few months' activity produced a new manual entitled *Army Transport Aviation — Combat Operations* to cover the basic techniques. In June 1956, Col Jay D. Vanderpool, Chief of the Army's Aviation School Combat Development Office, began a series of armament trials with contemporary helicopters. Types such as the H-19, H-34 and H-21 were modified to take a variety of machine gun, cannon, rocket and missile combinations for air firing tests. These gave comprehensive data on airframe stress, armament rigging methods and weapon accuracy and conclusively proved that armed helicopters were a practical proposition.

In 1952, midway through the Korean war, the United States Army drew up a hypothetical plan for the future deployment of helicopters, principally in the European and Middle Eastern theatres of operation. It included 12 helicopter battalions to form as and when suitable aircraft became available and, during these deliberations, the term 'airmobility' was coined. That word became the cornerstone of Army aviation, the ultimate aim of the Army being to deploy a fully mobile and independent force, equipped with its own 'organic' helicopters and able to airlift troops into battle zones quickly, supply and reinforce them and extract them once an objective had been secured. It was also thought possible that armed helicopters would protect such a force during the airlift operation. These 'gunships' would be able to respond to local, rapidly changing conditions when there probably would not be time to call in fixed-wing air support.

All this had never been done before and there was precious little hard evidence that it would work. Consequently, Army planners drew on every possible source for the answers they needed, particularly the events then taking place in Korea. They also looked closely at British and French heliborne operations in locations as diverse as Malaya and Algeria. French methods were of particular interest, as the Algerian war was the first conflict in which armed helicopters were used, albeit on an ad hoc basis.

Maj-Gen James M. Gavin was one of the US Army's earliest exponents of airmobility. He likened the helicopter to the cavalry horse of a bygone age, when the mounted soldier was the elite of armies otherwise composed of infantry. Cavalry, well trained in tactics, had two qualities that set it apart — freedom of movement and speed. Gavin imagined an air cavalry equipped with helicopters having both qualities in abundance.

Irrespective of the fact that the Army lacked the ideal helicopter for the purpose, it nevertheless set out

Early Designs

If the Korean war provided the military with much valuable information, it also gave US helicopter manufacturers the chance to observe the performance of their products under operational conditions. Among the observers was Lawrence D. Bell, the man who had founded the company that bore his name back in July 1935. Bell's President visited the war zone in 1953 and returned home justifiably proud of the rotorcraft's record. He stated that 'Korea advanced the development of the helicopter by 10 years'.

Bell Aircraft had grown considerably before and during World War 2, mainly by building fixed-wing fighters and bombers. The company had also developed helicopters in the early war years and it was during the design phase of the company's two-seat Model 30 that the research work of engineers Arthur Young and Bartram Kelley came to the attention of Lawrence Bell — he persuaded both men to join the company. When the Model 30 first flew, on 29 July 1943, it featured a stabiliser bar for the main rotor. This bar, the invention of Young, was set at right angles to the blades with a streamlined counterweight at each end — a device which was to become a hallmark of Bell helicopters for some time to come.

A helicopter division headed by Lawrence Bell was established in 1951 and with the famous Model 47 (H-13) the firm gained a wealth of useful data, not least in the mass production of helicopters. The developed Model 47H, Model 48 and others gave Bell experience in building bigger, multi-seat rotorcraft, all of them powered by piston engines. However, some research that started in the early 1950s in Stratford, Connecticut was to lead to an entirely new type of helicopter engine, the gas turbine.

That research was conducted by the Lycoming company under the leadership of Dr Anslem Franz, a member of the team responsible for the world's first production jet engine, the Junkers Jumo 004. Franz

Above:
The XH-40 was the prototype of the US Army's first turbine-powered helicopter, production versions of which were to revolutionise that service's aviation capability. *via Barry Wheeler*

Below:
This overhead view of one of the XH-40s shows salient features of the Huey prototypes, including the raised rotor head fairing, intake shape and extreme aft position of the elevators. *via Barry Wheeler*

had come to the USA under Operation 'Paperclip', the exodus of scientists from what became the eastern zone of Germany under Russian control. In 1952, the US Government recognised his work by awarding Lycoming a contract for a small gas turbine for observation aircraft. Adapted for installation in helicopters, this engine was the 600 shaft horsepower (shp) XT53.

The advantages of gas turbines over piston engines for helicopters are principally that they are lighter, they offer considerably more power and permit the use of simpler drive systems. A 'free' turbine or turboshaft engine also increases available cabin space as it can be mounted horizontally above the fuselage, whereas a piston engine invariably occupies valuable space inside the fuselage.

On 23 February 1955 the US Army awarded Bell Aircraft a contract for a new utility helicopter on the strength of a company design study submitted within an industry competition. Mission definition emphasised casualty evacuation (medevac) from the battlefield, with general duties and an instrument flying training capability secondary to that role. The specification called for an 8,000lb payload, a mission radius of 100 nautical miles (nm) at a sustained speed of 100kts IAS and the ability to hover out of ground effect at 6,000ft in temperatures of 95°C. Ideally, the helicopter had to have a fuselage small enough to be air-transportable by C-124 or C-130.

Bell's design was the Model 204, or XH-40 under the USAF funding and designation system prevailing at the time for all Army aircraft. A single-engined helicopter of all-metal monocoque construction using

magnesium, the XH-40 was powered by the Lycoming XT53-L-1 turboshaft rated at 700shp. A two-blade semi-rigid main rotor of 44ft diameter was fitted, each blade being of extruded aluminium spars. Blade stability was achieved by the Bell-designed system and each one was interchangeable. An internal honeycomb structure was used for the two-blade tail rotor, which was mounted atop a swept-back tailfin. At the base of the fin were elevators integrally linked to the cyclic control.

The XH-40 was 42ft 8in long, skid supported and provided with two twin wheel units for ground towing. The machine's low silhouette fuselage was bulged outwards at the centre section to give a distinctive 'tadpole' shape. Crew access was by outwards-opening car type doors on each side, with main cabin doors sliding back on fuselage runners.

The knee-height cabin floor enabled easy loading of equipment, there being 140sq ft of floor space aft of the pilot and co-pilot's seats. Up to eight persons could be carried in place of freight, occupying the three seats behind the crew and a five-man bench seat at the cabin rear. In the medevac role the aircraft could acommodate four stretchers tiered along the cabin sides in place of the bench seat.

The prototype XH-40 (55-4459) made its maiden flight on 22 October 1956, in the hands of Bell test pilot Floyd Carlson. Early performance figures showed the aircraft to have a useful speed range between 124mph cruising and 138mph maximum;

Below:
Three-view of the YH-40 design. *Bell*

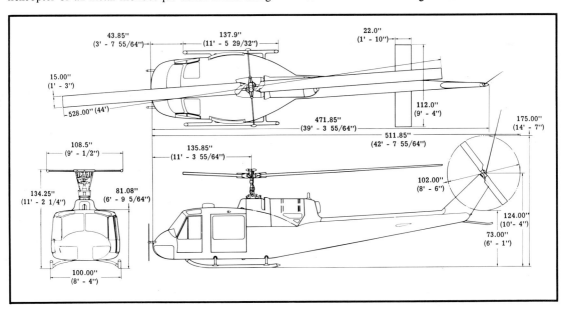

Above:
Bell refined the design and made changes to the pre-production YH-40s. This is the second one to fly, s/n 56-6724. *via Barry Wheeler*

inclined climb rate was 2,350ft/min and service ceiling was 17,500ft. Range with 165gal of JP4 fuel was 212 miles. Empty weight was low at 3,692lb and gross weight loaded a still-modest 5,650lb.

Bell built three XH-40s powered by the 700shp engine, followed by six YH-40 evaluation aircraft. These latter machines differed in having a 770shp T53 engine and some revisions to the original configuration, including reduction of the number of engine cooling panels from 10 to four and elimination of a bulbous fairing around the main rotor shaft. The turbine air intake was reshaped and the elevators repositioned some feet forward of their original lower fin position.

The changes to the YH-40s were mainly the results of exhaustive US Army testing, which was completed in June 1957, just over a year before the delivery of the

final pre-production aircraft in August 1958. All the XH-40s and a single YH-40 were retained by Bell. Of the other five, three were used by the Army for trials at Fort Rucker, one went to the USAF for evaluation at Edwards AFB, and one was used for new type testing at Eglin AFB.

All XH-40s were redesignated as XHU-1s in 1956, although the prototypes are still generally known by their Air Force designations. The first prototype was presented to the US Army Museum at Fort Rucker in 1961 by Continental Army Command, where it joined other historic UH/AH-1s in honourable retirement.

The Model 204 was the first Bell helicopter designed and built at the Hurst plant at Fort Worth in Texas, which opened in 1951. The company remained part of Bell Aircraft throughout the early development of the UH-1 and did not become a separate entity until 1 January 1957 with the founding of Bell Helicopter. The first flight of the firm's most successful design was tempered by the death of Lawrence Bell — 'Larry' to all friends and colleagues — on 20 October two days before the first flight of the XH-40.

Right:
The first YH-40 (56-6723) became the Model 533 high speed test vehicle to explore compound helicopter configuration.
via Barry Wheeler

Below:
Bell's Fort Worth production line showing how (in all cases but one) UH-1 front sections had the engine installed before the tailboom was fitted. *Bell*

2.
Combat Classroom

In line with US Army policy of naming its aircraft after American Indian tribes, the new utility helicopter became the Iroquois. Not the most familiar Indian name, open to various pronunciations, this was quickly changed to 'Huey' by Army personnel. Derived from the machine's original HU designation and 'Baby Huey' of cartoon fame, the popular designation survived the type's redesignation as UH-1 in 1962 and became so widely used that Bell eventually perpetuated it by stamping it on every helicopter that left the works — 'Bell' went on the left anti-torque or 'rudder' pedal in service slang, and 'Huey' on the right one.

The nine XH and YH-40 prototype/evaluation aircraft were followed by nine UH-1s. The cost of these 18 machines was a record low at $28.7million including engines.

Bell initiated production of the UH-1A in the spring of 1959, a US Army order having been placed on 13 March. Deliveries of the first of 173 HU-1As began in June and production was completed by March 1961. Similar to the UH-1, the A model had a gross weight of 7,200lb (3,924lb empty) and was powered by a T53-L-1 engine of 770shp derated to 680shp. Fitted with dual controls and blind flying instruments, 14 became TH-1As for the Army Aviation School.

The concurrent development of the HU-1B, the first large-scale production Huey featuring a number of important changes, saw five A models used in flight testing (including the redesignated XH-1A used for grenade launcher, rocket and machine gun evaluation). The first HU-1B flew on 27 April 1960; the powerplant was initially the T53-L-5 of 960shp although the L-9 or L-11 engines of 1,100shp were introduced during production to give the Bravo model a small but significant performance boost. The B model had a rotor mast 13in taller than that of the A model without underslung blade weights. Blade chord was 21in rather than the previous 14in; aluminium honeycomb replaced spars as in the HU-1A, the weights being moved to the top of the blade grips. The lengthened mast gave a less critical centre of gravity range and enabled the HU-1B to increase cabin loading by some 50%. Gross weight went up to 8,500lb. The honeycomb construction gave a better strength-to-weight ratio of the main rotor blades and

Below:
One of the first production batch of UH-1As, 57-6099 had the 700shp T53-L-1A engine. Note the underslung blade weights which helped identify the early model Hueys. *Bell*

interchangeability was improved, as was control of blade contour during manufacture. The result was a far more flexible and reliable aircraft which was to become the mainstay of US forces in the early years of the Vietnam war.

The majority of the HU-1A and early B models were used for training by the Army, which was keen to integrate the HU-1 into its airmobility concept. It did so with a new generation of warrant officer pilots, men who entered the Army specifically to fly helicopters under a far-sighted programme begun in 1951. Also open to selected enlisted personnel who trained as pilots and were given their warrants on completion of training, this programme eliminated the former requirement that individuals could take pilot training only if they had reached commissioned rank in one of

Above:
The first example of the fourth UH-1A batch was used for the 1960 series of record flights. Clearly marked for the purpose, 59-1607 is seen in flight near Fort Worth. *Bell via Bruce Robertson*

Below:
Also from a first production batch, but this time of the Bravo model, 60-3606 shows the revised rotor head which was 13in taller than that of the Alpha model. *Bell*

the Army branches that were authorised aircraft. A speeding up process to provide crews for the large number of helicopters the Army was then in the process of ordering, the warrant officer pilot programme eventually provided enough crews for the SE Asian commitment.

Crews were quick to grasp the potential of the HU-1 over previous US Army helicopters; there were some reservations about the A model, but the Bravo's improvements refined the design to such an extent that it well deserved the accolade 'Cadillac of helicopters'. Army chiefs now had the main means of airmobility at their disposal for although the HU-1 was only one element of the airborne army, it was by far the most important. The Huey's capability in performing every type of mission within its weight category, from rapid casualty evacuation to battlefield command and control, set new standards for army aviation that would be emulated — though rarely on the American scale — by military forces around the world. And many of those forces would do so with the very same type of helicopter.

As the first production HU-1s entered US Army service, the war in which the type was to win its spurs continued to bring hardship and suffering to the peoples of Vietnam and in the spring of 1962 the first UH-1s were sent there. With the establishment of Military Assistance Command Vietnam (MACV) on 11 December 1962, the US Army prepared to commit helicopters to Vietnam in unit strength to boost the number of machines available to Government forces. At that time types such as the Sikorsky H-19, H-21, H-34 and H-37 were employed as transports by the South Vietnamese, supported by American advisors, including helicopter crews. These 'first generation' helicopters had begun to suffer losses as Communist incursion into the south increased in the late 1950s and early 1960s.

Above:
A UH-1B on slung load tests for the US Army Aviation Board. While the Huey could easily handle such a task, in service the job was usually handled by the heavy-lift helicopters. *via Barry Wheeler*

Left:
Air America, the CIA airline, operated a wide variety of fixed-wing aircraft and helicopters, including Hueys. Active in SE Asia long before any official US presence there, the CIA had a number of UH-1s marked like this dark blue and silver C model, N8514F. *Joe Turner via R. L. Ward*

13

A Marine helicopter squadron began operations in Vietnam early in 1962 and American crews operated within the loosely defined command structure under quite stringent 'rules of engagement', flying missions for the South Vietnamese Army. This early learning period was summed up as the 'art of the possible'. It was a less than ideal way to prove the effectiveness of airmobility; prevailing conditions blunted the efforts of superior forces against an elusive, cunning enemy able to use local knowledge to maximum advantage. Carrying Vietnamese officers familiar with local terrain and conditions, helicopters had to wait for the enemy to show hostile intentions before attempting to land a fire team. Therefore it often happened that government forces arrived at a hamlet or village to find the dwellings in flames, the occupants butchered and the enemy melted away into the countryside.

Helicopters achieved some successes however, and the Viet Cong began not only to suffer casualties but realise that its clandestine operations were increasingly at risk — a risk proportionate to the growing air capability of the South Vietnamese and their allies. Captured personnel, moved quickly to base areas by helicopters, confirmed this fact and under interrogation yielded valuable information that assisted the planning of future anti-guerilla operations.

As the ARVN (the South Vietnamese army) gained confidence in airmobility, carefully planned assaults were made by forces up to battalion size. Inevitably this challenge was met by bolder Viet Cong action against both forces on the ground and by ambush of

helicopters, particularly when they were committed to landing and at their most vulnerable. Despite pre-assault fixed-wing air strikes by the South Vietnamese Air Force, it became increasingly obvious that the helicopter transports needed more protection through localised air support, particularly during the landing phase.

The first Bell UH-1s in Vietnam were the A model air ambulances of the 57th Medical Detachment (Helicopter Ambulance), which arrived in April 1962. The first armed machines soon followed, in September. These were the first of 15 HU-1As of the Utility Tactical Transport Helicopter Company (UTTHC), tasked to test the helicopter gunship under actual combat conditions. They were fitted with standard infantry machine guns and rockets bolted on to the skids. The most usual combination was a belt fed .30cal short recoil Browning M-2 attached to the forward skid on each side, with up to eight launching tubes for 80mm rockets on the aft one. The weapons were located on the bow-shaped supporting cross tubes of the skids and were fixed to fire forward by the pilot.

Below:
The first UH-1s in Vietnam were the A models of the 57th Medical Detachment (Helicopter Ambulance), as shown by 58-2081 and 58-3035 parked alongside CH-21s. The 57th stayed in Vietnam for 11 years and 'wrote the book' on medevac for other units to follow.
Bill Hardy via Pete Harlem

Direct fire support weapons required extensive flight testing. This B model carries the XM-3 sub-system consisting of two 24-tube launchers for 2.75in folding fin aircraft rockets.
via Barry Wheeler

The work of UTTHC was monitored by ACTIV — Army Concept Team in Vietnam — established in Saigon on 6 November 1962. Although concerned with other aspects of combat, ACTIV was able to make a comprehensive study of armed helicopter operations during the period from 16 October 1962 to 15 March 1963. Results were obtained from both combat crews and the personal involvement of ACTIV evaluators on missions, the programme being made more representative by the fact that the armed helicopters were used only on actual missions.

Initially the task of the armed helicopters was fire protection for CH-21 Shawnee transport helicopters during an assault, together with fire protection at landing zones. The established 'fire only if fired on' rule prevailed until February 1963 when it was revised to permit helicopters to engage forces clearly showing hostile intentions.

Based at Saigon's Tan Son Nhut Airport, the UTTHC primarily supported the 57th, 33rd and 93rd Light Helicopter Companies, all equipped with the H-21 and operating mainly in the III and IV Corps Tactical Zones in the southernmost part of South Vietnam. But from April 1963, a detachment of UH-1As was sent further north to provide escort to Marine HU-34s in I Corps area.

More muscle was added to UTTHC inventory in November 1962, when 11 UH-1Bs arrived to begin operations. These machines had the first factory-installed armament kits based on a 'universal' Emerson turret mounting on each side of the fuselage aft of the cargo doors. Hydraulically powered, the XM-6E2 (later simply M-6) was a quad mount for four 7.62mm M-60 machine guns which could be rotated through 75° downwards and 82° in azimuth. They were fired either by the co-pilot/gunner using a flexible sighting station from the left seat, or by the pilot using a Mk VIII sight and operating the weapons as fixed armament firing forwards only. This flexible gun system was the basis for most subsequent Huey armament combinations operated by the flight crew, the turrets incorporating racks for a wide combination

15

of rocket pods and launchers mounted either above or below the turrets. An equally wide range of armament, particularly larger calibre guns, was cabin-mounted and operated by the Huey's crew chief or door gunner. In addition there was a great variety of special installations adopted by many 'in country' units.

Experience showed that the escort role for the gunships could be divided into en route, approach, and landing zone (LZ) phases. In the first, the formation generally proceeded at an altitude safe from small arms fire, typically 1,500ft. In the second the force employed nap-of-the-earth cover several miles from the LZ; and thirdly, the escorts dropped to 100-200ft to suppress enemy fire throughout the transport landings. Although most effective in the third phase, the escorts were then at their most vulnerable, as they came well within range of small arms fire. Nevertheless, the results of the UTTHC trial appeared to well justify the investment in gunship escorts. During 1,779 combat support sorties in the five-month period, 11 armed helicopters were hit by hostile fire for an estimated 246 Viet Cong casualties. Only one UH-1B was seriously damaged and none was shot down.

A result of UTTHC's work was the decision to convert helicopter companies destined for Vietnam to a new airmobile organisation whereby each one would consist of a single armed platoon of eight UH-1Bs and two transport platoons, also with eight B models each. As the armed Hueys would not carry troops, needing to give all available cabin space to weapons and ammunition, discretion had to be exercised in the distance they flew from the main transport force while it was en route to a landing zone. If they strayed too far, the escorts were in danger, due to their heavier weight and slower speed, of being left behind by the main force when it landed — at the very time when their firepower could make the difference between success and failure. Such 'lessons' laid the groundwork for improving command structure and helped the development of helicopters and weapons. It had become clear that transport helicopter operations in Vietnam ran a grave risk without armed escorts 'riding shotgun' all the way — and that there was a requirement for a faster escort ship.

Some Inter-Service Rivalry

While the US Army was sold on the armed helicopter, other branches of the US armed services had a somewhat cooler attitude and the early 1960s were to see a long drawn out, and at times bitter, argument to the effect that the Army was over-stretching previously agreed limits on organic air support. The Air Force was particularly vocal in its disapproval and made its first attempt to regulate the role of armed helicopters in December 1962. A document was issued which stated that gunships had exceeded an undertaking to lay down fire 'one minute before the transport helicopters landed and one minute after the last one departed'. Not surprisingly, this arrangement proved unworkable in practice and the Army constantly sought more flexible guidelines for its field commanders to interpret under prevailing conditions.

Below:
A unique civil Huey is this all-black example operated by the US Customs in Florida on anti-smuggling patrols.
US Customs

In particular it sought discretion to call in Air Force close air support as and when commanders wanted it — and to use helicopter support at all other times. Somewhat ironically, considering how well the UTTHC's armed helicopter support had been received during their detachment, the Marines initially sided with the USAF. The Corps' seeming lack of enthusiasm for armed helicopters hid a fundamental fear that purchase of such aircraft would cut its traditional fixed-wing air support budget. But with actual combat results to back their arguments, Army commanders won the day. The Marines were to change their attitude and the Air Force was to reach a compromise. Armed helicopters would not only stay — they would be freed of any operational restrictions on their assigned missions. The Air Force's criticism, founded on supposed erosion of its close support role, came to a head in 1966 when it argued forcibly for the transfer of Army operated Caribou transports in return for a binding agreement that the Army would be responsible for its own helicopter close support.

The First Non-US Hueys

The first country outside America to place an order for the Huey was Australia, which paid $4million for eight UH-1Bs for the RAAF on 17 April 1961. The second aircraft type to be serialled under the third new Australian series adopted in 1960 (the first being another Bell helicopter, the Sioux) this initial batch of RAAF Iroquois was intended to equip two new army co-operation squadrons, Nos 5 and 9. Identified with the prefix A2- followed by the last three digits of the constructor's number, all eight aircraft actually went to No 9 Squadron at RAAF Base Williamstown, New South Wales for search and rescue duties. The first two aircraft were airlifted from the USA to Australia by C-130 in September 1962 and in November No 9 Squadron moved to Fairbairn. An additional eight UH-1Bs were ordered in December.

It was somewhat fortuitous that the RAAF had ordered the same utility helicopter as the US Army, for in March 1966 No 9 (UH) Squadron was selected as part of the Australian commitment in Vietnam. The unit departed for SE Asia aboard the carried HMAS *Sydney* on 25 May and was installed at Vung Tau airfield by 6 June. The main party of the squadron arrived on 12 June and the next day No 9's Hueys went into action. The squadron was not then fully operational having had only two of its helicopters fitted with armoured seats, but an ammunition supply flight was successfully carried out.

From that small beginning, No 9 Squadron went on to write an impressive chapter in RAAF history; the UH-1B was soon joined in Vietnam by Delta models and both built an enviable reputation of close support to Australian ground forces 'doing their bit' in a confusing, frustrating war. Using the callsigns 'Bushranger' and 'Albatross' throughout, the unit spent $4\frac{1}{2}$ years in the war zone, flying its last mission on 19 November 1971. It had then logged 223,487 operational sorties for the loss of five aircraft.

Below:
The first overseas customer for the UH-1B was Australia. No 9 (SAR) Squadron RAAF received A2-384, the first of eight ordered. *Eric Allen*

Above:
Also in the first RAAF batch was UH-1B A2-387, lost in an accident near Captain's Flat, New South Wales in November 1968. *Eric Allen*

Below:
Bravo models also served the Australian Navy's No 723 Squadron at Nowra, New South Wales (HMAS *Albatross*). Some remain today, the paint scheme of blue and white having been used since first deliveries in 1964. Previously serialled 63-8659, N9-881 was written off in June 1968. *Eric Allen*

3.
Asian Deployment

In the late 1950s and 1960s, the US helicopter industry indulged in extensive research to extend the boundaries of rotorcraft performance and design using both production machines and experimental models. Of particular interest was the development of a practical compound helicopter. Within this time frame, the US military initiated numerous projects by most of the leading manufacturers, Bell included. In 1959 the Army's Transportation Research Command (TRECOM) launched a programme aimed at determining practical upper speed limits for helicopters, and began with a modified UH-1B. Bell used YH-40 s/n 56-6723 as the basis for the conversion, and gave it a new model number, 533.

The machine flew for the first time on 10 August 1962. A general cleaning up was carried out to reduce drag, this including mounting the cabin doors on piano wire hinges, streamlining the landing skids and fairing the rotor head. The Bell stabilizer bar was removed and a variable-tilt rotor mast substituted to maintain a low-drag horizontal attitude to the fuselage. Redesign of the engine air intake duct resulted in two flush intakes on the side of the new rotor fairing to increase power available at the main rotor, an accomplishment assisted by cambering and enlarging the vertical tail. Tests in the NASA's Ames wind tunnel revealed the UH-1B's equivalent flatplate area to have been reduced from 25sq ft to about 11sq ft. Flight tests at Forth Worth in late 1962 translated these figures into a much improved performance, and in March 1963 the Model 533 flew at 175mph, compared with 135mph for a standard UH-1B in level flight.

Progressive modifications to the same machine produced a simple compound helicopter, the changes centring around advanced rotors, the addition of jet engines, and wings. The first tests were with three-bladed rotors of various degrees of rigidity (gimballed, semi-rigid and rigid). Speeds up to 210mph were attained by adding two Continental J69-T-9 turbojets,

each of 920lb thrust, to either side of the fuselage. Breaking the 200kt barrier was a 'first' for helicopters, this speed being achieved for the first time on 15 October 1964. A second milestone was reached on 6 April 1965, when the Model 533 flew at 250mph in level attitude and 254mph in a shallow dive. Boosting the primary powerplant with turbojets also enabled manoeuvrability to be maintained at high speed. Flights included 2g turns and 60° banking at around 200mph, and a Mach number of 0.985 was recorded by the advancing blades of the rotor, which had tapering tips of 6% thickness. A subsequent phase of the Model 533 programme was the installation of two P&W JT12A-3 turbojets of 3,300lb static thrust each, at the end of short stub wings. First flying in this configuration in 1968, the machine gradually recorded still higher speeds and in May 1969, Bell announced that 316mph had been attained.

Bell's extensive research and development support programme for the UH-1 included a reconfigured UH-1A designated RH-2 (Research Helicopter 2). Fitted out as a flying laboratory, it featured new instrumentation and control systems operated electronically, and carried a high resolution radar in a large fairing above the flight deck. This enabled the pilot to detect obstacles ahead of the aircraft in bad visibility. A single B model was also used for testing and was given the designation NUH-1B. In fact the short-fuselage UH-1B was the basis for subsequent models used by the Army, Air Force and Marines, progressive improvements being made directly as a result of Vietnam experience. It was mainly a need to obtain more lift capability and performance from the B model in the hot and humid conditions of the war zone that led to the first of these, the UH-1C.

More fuel capacity — 242gal instead of 165gal in the B model — was provided, the powerplant being the T53-L-11 engine driving the Bell 540 'door hinge' rotor system. This employed blades of 27in chord instead of the standard chord of 18in in previous models and incorporated a single-piece flex-beam rotor head that gave the Charlie model near aerobatic handling. Vertical fin chord was increased and deeply cambered 7° from the centreline to provide anti-torque movement to the right to unload the tail rotor during high speed manoeuvres. Reverse airfoil synchronised elevators replaced the conventional airfoil with full-span spoiler. The pitot tube and FM homing aerial mountings were removed from the nose and repositioned on the roof, and two white position lights instead of one were mounted on each side of the vertical tailboom.

With their significantly better performance, the majority of UH-1Cs were built as gunships, able to carry the full range of armament sub-systems without

a performance penalty which could possibly jeopardise the safety of those 'slicks' they were tasked to escort. First deliveries of the 749 UH-1Cs built were made to the Army in June 1965.

Tactics

As more UH-1s became available in Vietnam — there were some 250 on hand by September 1964 — the Army further developed the basic guidelines of deploying armed helicopters to best effect. Responsibility for engaging targets was vested in the escort leader, who maintained constant radio contact with his force. Wherever possible, suppressive fire was opened at the maximum range of the Hueys' weapons, starting with guns and following with rockets. Various formations were adopted so that as the lead helicopter completed its target run, the next was in position to follow through. Such was the flexibility of helicopter-mounted weapons that crews could manoeuvre freely and select the most effective and safe attack profiles. Briefings identified known concentrations of enemy forces before a mission was mounted, and the procedures to be adopted by escorts and transports during en route and landing phases laid down. The escort leader usually relinquished command of his force after the troops had landed, and handed this over to the ground commander, who would direct the helicopters on to points of enemy resistance, having first marked out friendly areas to avoid casualties from his own air strikes. Depending on how long the escorts remained in the vicinity of the landing zone, they were also placed under the command of the transport force commander during en route and landing phases.

Related to the size of the force, a stepped 'V' formation was found to be the most versatile and easy to control, permitting landing in the minimum time without bunching. Each transport flew at about 45° to the side and rear of the leader, high enough to avoid his rotor wash. At the same altitude as the transport force, there would be the escort and a reconnaissance force of four to five UH-1s preceding the transports by one to five minutes. The remaining escorts flanked the transports in trail formation and, if available, further gunships were positioned at the rear of the transport formation to engage any targets below it. Given the right conditions — principally a fire-free landing zone and good, firm terrain — it was reckoned that a 12-ship transport force could unload in an average of two minutes.

Commanders usually attempted to land all the transport helicopters at once, providing the LZ was large enough and the terrain firm enough to support their weight. When it was not the transports got as low

as possible to allow the troops to jump off, using the skids as foot holds. On occasion, troops also swung down on 120ft ropes or rope ladders, a technique known as 'rapelling' in the US armed forces and as abseiling in others, including Britain's.

To lessen the risk of ambushes, return routes were varied as much as possible; all helicopters also departed at the same time to avoid the enemy concentrating fire on one machine. Last to leave the scene were the reconnaissance aircraft.

Such was the nature of the conflict in South Vietnam that US/ARVN helicopter assaults could not always count on surprise, invariably essential if an operation was to be successful. MAAG (Military Assistance Advisory Group) therefore decided to form rapid response forces to undertake operations at short notice with the minimum of planning and briefing. These were Eagle Flights, initially attached to a small number of helicopter units, but soon adopted by most of them by November 1964. Each flight consisted of an armed Huey command and control (C&C) ship carrying the ARVN troop commander and US

Army aviation commander; seven Huey 'slicks' carried the troops, five armed Hueys acted as the escort and one took care of the 'Dust off' or medevac duty. The Eagle Flight was placed on continuous strip alert or was airborne when the call to action came and served to bridge a gap between the larger assaults and later Air Cavalry missions. Eagle Flights often initiated their own operations, teamed with other flights for a more powerful assault which still required quick reaction, and responded to calls for assistance from units already in the field.

An Eagle Flight usually included UH-1Bs and UH-1Cs armed with the M-5 armament sub-system consisting of a nose-mounted M-75 automatic grenade launcher. Fired by the co-pilot's flexible sighting system, the launcher was fed by a magazine containing 150 or 315 rounds. It was considered to be one of the most effective weapons carried by armed Hueys, a machine so armed being widely referred to as a 'Frog'. As well as flying a wide variety of missions involving a small number of aircraft, two being the minimum for mutual protection, armed Bravo and Charlie models were teamed together or with A-1 Skyraiders for

Left:
Training at Camp Pendleton Marine Base includes the art of rapelling. Here troops are using a UH-1E as their 'jump off' platform. *USMC*

Below left:
There were many local armament modifications to helicopters in Vietnam. This Huey has the SM-158 launcher topped by a .50cal machine gun with boxed rather than belted ammunition. *Joe Turner via R. L. Ward*

Below:
The M-21 armament system combined a 7.62mm XM-134 minigun and an XM-158 rocket launcher.
Joe Turner via R. L. Ward

Below:
The 'Big Friends' of the Vietnam war were the CH-47 Chinooks and CH-54 Skycranes. The mighty Chinook was quite capable of moving a damaged Huey to a repair base, and saved many helicopters that would otherwise have been lost. This CH-47 is uplifting a UH-1B of the 'Outlaws', the 175th Aviation Company. *Boeing-Vertol*

Bottom:
Friend in need. A downed UH-1C 'Hog' is located and its position noted for lifting out, repair and sending back into the line. *via Bruce Robertson*

'Hunter-Killer' sorties. An Army Huey would locate and attack a target and the Air Force A-1 would follow up with its extensive ordnance to finish the job.

Probably the most famous helicopter units operating in Vietnam were those of the Air Cavalry Troops. Armed Hueys were the 'Guns' section of an integrated Air Cav force, the Red Team. Flying with a White (Scout) Team, the Guns became a Pink Team. The scouts flew low, alert for any enemy contact, while the gunships flew above, awaiting the call to attack. Numbers varied, but one or two pairs was the norm, either with or without a command and control ship to direct operations. Any target that could not be dealt with on the spot could be taken out by the Blue Team — aero rifle platoons or ARPs which deployed rapidly with troop transports.

Formation of the 1st Cavalry Division (Airmobile) on 1 July 1965 was the culmination of the original air assault concept first mooted in the 1950s and given substance at Fort Benning, Georgia in the summer of 1964. Successfully evaluated in a massive exercise against the 82nd Airborne Division in late 1964, the 1st Cav became operational within a year of formation. It was the first large Army unit tasked with tactical warfare in inhospitable terrain and was bloodied in action in the Pleiku campaign of October-November 1965.

Tactics were pioneered by the 1st Squadron, 9th Cavalry Regiment, which arrived in the An Khe area in August 1965. A unique unit, 1/9 acted as the 'eyes and ears' of the division. Of battalion size, it was entirely mobile, its inventory including nearly 100 helicopters, about a quarter of the 400 or so in 1st Cavalry Division itself. As with most cavalry divisions, the 1st was composed of A, B and C Troops, each with an aero scout platoon with OH-13s, a weapons platoon (UH-1Bs), and an aero rifle platoon of UH-1D infantry transports. Each troop was roughly the size of a regular Army assault helicopter company in terms of personnel and number of aircraft. In addition there was an HQ troop which provided maintenance, logistic and administrative support, and D Troop, a ground reconnaissance unit.

The rapidly increasing number of helicopter units in Vietnam created a need for a more comprehensive command structure. Consequently, the 1st Aviation Brigade was activated on 25 May 1966. It encompassed seven aviation groups, 15 battalions plus four provisional battalions, and four Air Cavalry squadrons. In addition to combat sorties, UH-1s flew 'ash and trash' missions, the routine, fetch and carry sorties that were part and parcel of the indirect support of US and South Vietnamese forces and the civilian population. On the battlefield, the medevac 'Dust off' missions had by March 1973 moved some 390,000 Army patients to a medical facility. No less than 100

UH-1s were engaged primarily on ambulance flights in Vietnam by 1968.

As the war reached a peak in terms of American personnel engaged, questions began to be asked on the number of helicopters lost in action. Some none-too-well-informed quarters implied that these were uneconomically high and although taken alone they seemed excessive, they were not always compared with the extremely high sortie level. Since the war, published figures for US Army helicopter losses include these totals: lost in South Vietnam 1961-71 — 2,066; total losses, including those over North Vietnam — 4,642. Apart from 10 lost over the North, there were more non-combat losses, at 2,566. It should be stressed that 'lost' refers only to aircraft shot down or crashed, the figures not including the many that were subsequently recovered. Not all of them are of course, UH-1s, but the totals can be taken to be Bell helicopters in about two-thirds (probably more) of the combat and non-combat totals. On the other side of the coin, there were 7,547,000 assault sorties and 3,952,000 attack sorties, the majority of which were conducted by UH-1s, during the period 1966-71. To these figures can be added 21,098,000 'other' sorties and pure cargo sorties, bringing the total for the period to 36,145,000.

It has been estimated that between 40% and 50% of UH-1 losses were as a result of fuel fires; research during and since the Vietnam war has concentrated on finding an effective fire suppressing agent, not only for helicopter fuel, but aviation fuel in general. Relatively few helicopters were lost by being blown apart in mid-air, but a loss could occur if small calibre fire penetrated fuel cells.

The Vietnam war also brought forth a comprehensive 'sub-vocabulary' of abbreviations, nicknames and slang to describe military operations, weapons, conditions and people. Helicopter warfare generated its share of this jargon, some of which has been used here, and which, in the main, had a practical purpose. Being succinct and widely understood it did, for example, cut down time spent on radio transmissions when speedily-passed messages could make the difference between life and death. The term 'Huey' itself was created before the war, but combat produced 'slick' for a troop transport helicopter; 'Cobras' were the early armed UH-1s and later the AH-1 — also widely known as 'snakes': 'Dust-off' was the universal term for a medevac flight. 'Medevac' itself being equally popular and used as a call sign by helicopter ambulance units. Both became general terms. A 'Hog' was a rocket-equipped gunship with the M-3 armament, a 'Frog' one with the M-5 grenade-launcher system — this weapon in turn being known as the 'Thumper', 'Chunker', 'Clunker' or 'Blooper' due to its distinctive sound when fired.

A Day in Vietnam

Not untypical of the UH-1B's performance in Vietnam was the story of the 1,000th example built, written as a first-person account in the form of a letter from the helicopter — 'Mr Huey'. Without revealing details of the unit, personnel, locations and so on, it nevertheless showed how the Army employed its primary utility helicopter in the war zone. The gist of it follows:

The aircraft was assigned to an assault helicopter company along with 22 other slicks and eight gunships. The company commander was a major on his second Vietnam tour and the Huey's crew was two pilots and a crew chief who flew on each mission to operate the M-60 machine gun installed in the right rear door, plus a gunner for the left M-60.

At the time the pilot of this particular Huey was an FNG — 'frightened new guy' — the term applied to Army pilots and other personnel during their first two months in Vietnam. The man in charge was the aircraft commander, a warrant officer posted directly to Vietnam, from flight school. A veteran of 10 months combat flying, he had been trained under the close supervision of old-timers like the company commander.

The crew chief was, by normal Army aviation standards, pretty green. He had graduated from a mechanic's course in the States, went directly to Vietnam and had been looking after this particular UH-1 ever since. It was a solid crew of professionals, none of whom was over 23.

But the helicopter was the real veteran of the theatre, having been there 18 months and flown over 1,800 hours. A soldier's Vietnam duty was one year; the Huey was deemed to have completed a tour at about 2,200 hours. Then it would probably be overhauled and sent back for another.

A typical day for the crew was an 06.00 lift-off before first light with a flight of 10 slicks and four gunships for a combat assault. The flight proceeded in loose formation to the pick-up point. The landing area was in this case what remained of a dirt road, with holes, craters and obstacles on all sides. One of the great hazards on this type of operation was obscurement by billowing dust, which could cause pilots to lose ground reference while trying to land next to other aircraft and people.

The final planning state, last minute co-ordination for the mission and loading of the aircraft was done in about 30 minutes. Then all was ready for the first combat assault of the day. As the take-off area was small, sand and dust were a serious problem, so each helicopter lifted off independently and joint formation in flight. On reaching the holding point the formation circled for about 10 minutes, during which time crews could see artillery fire going into the objective area, followed by air strikes by US fighters. The gunships were holding just at the edge of the objective ready to offer local fire support after the heavy strikes stopped.

The artillery fire count-down came over the radio. The mission commander scheduled departure from the holding point to arrive at the landing zone seconds after the suppressive fire had ceased. As the helicopters departed the holding area, the formation tightened up — and so did everybody in it . . .

Departure was reported to the mission commander, flying in a Huey 1,500ft above the LZ. At one minute out, the air mission commander ordered the gunships to cease suppressive fire while one gunship marked the LZ with a smoke grenade. The gunship leader dropped the grenade at the best landing point for the lead slick. The air mission commander called 'Smoke is out'.

The commander of the lead slick answered 'I have your purple smoke'. Adopted to assure positive identification and foil enemy attempts at decoying formations by laying his own smoke, this procedure was varied to avoid an ambush.

Three minutes before landing; as the formation of lift ships headed for the LZ and accordingly tightened up its flight pattern, the gunships took station slightly behind and on both sides. Last-minute instructions from the lead pilot ended with: 'Force trim on and shoulder harness locked'.

The radio net, which had carried constant chatter on final corrections, courses to fly and instructions to the gunships, suddenly became silent. The next words were the lead pilot calling the distance in metres: '1,000 out'; '500 out'. Flying into the LZ, the silence was eerie. Everyone waited to hear if the helicopters would draw fire.

Right.
Boosting the basic M-6 armament system with twin door-mounted M-60s, this UH-1B in Vietnam also carries a seven-round rocket pod on the turret station. *via R. L. Ward*

A sudden explosion of noise. Door gunners of the slicks placed fire on the three edges of the LZ and the gunships started pouring rockets into possible enemy locations.

It turned out to be a 'hot' landing zone. Radio silence was broken. One pilot reported, 'I am drawing fire from that hut next to the canal'.

Number two gunship responded with 'I'm on it'.

The fire teams on the left began to draw fire while making their suppressive pass during the landing. Over the radio another gunship reported automatic weapons fire from the other side of the canal. He advised, 'Break right on departure and we'll cover you'.

The 10 lift ships settled in and the troops dismounted while the gunships flew a tight circle, covering the departing lift ships. The lead commander of the slicks called '10 in and 10 out — give me your damage report'. Each Huey responded in sequence. Seven reported 'No hits', three 'Hit but all gauges reading normal'. No great damage.

All aircraft made it safely back to the pick-up point, where each one was checked before loading troops for a second lift. The first troops had secured the LZ and for the next hour more men were lifted in. This done, the Hueys returned to a refuelling and rearming point to await further orders.

Refuelling and rearming was a practised, precision drill. In tight formation the Hueys would fly to a secure base in their operational area where two rows

of miniports (helipads) were arranged 15 to a row. The first four had ammunition racks and a fuel bladder and looked much like an octopus from above. Each helicopter would flare out to a hover, turn 90° and set down. The crew chief and gunner leapt out first to open the door for the pilots. The crew chief then refuelled the aircraft with the engine running while the pilot watched the gauges and the gunner rearmed both M-60s. The whole operation could be completed and the flight back in the air in less than five minutes.

Our crew relaxed for an hour. Then came the word that the company was released. Each aircraft commander then had a list of individual ash and trash missions to perform for the rest of the day. As our Huey took off on the first of these, a Mayday call

Below:
Bushwacking Bushranger. One of No 9 Squadron RAAF's D model gunships going in on a target with the port minigun blazing. The door gunner of A2-773 waits his turn to open up with his twin M-60s. 'Bushranger' was one of the Squadron's callsigns in Vietnam. *Bell*

came over the emergency net. A helicopter was going down near the base with mechanical trouble. The aircraft commander responded immediately with 'On the way'.

The Huey landed just behind the other helicopter and found the pilot with a broken arm and the gunner with possible internal injuries. As the first on the scene the Huey crew's job was to extract the crew and retrieve the weapons. Two gunships had also answered the Mayday call and were circling the downed machine, alert for any signs of the enemy.

With the rescued crew aboard, the Huey took off with the aircraft commander calling on the designated medical evacuation channel. He was told which medical unit to contact. The medics asked detailed questions about the casualties, to be ready to receive them as soon as the Huey touched down.

The second ash and trash mission was to pick up an engineer for a reconnaissance. He would have liked, in order to get a close look at the roads and bridges maintained by engineers, to fly at about 10ft altitude and 20kt IAS. But the aircraft commander, feeling that

kind of thing to be non-habit forming, preferred 1,500ft and 100kt.

The road recon was uneventful and the engineer next decided to visit a unit working on a bridge. There was no helicopter landing pad at the site so the Huey crew chose the only fairly level spot and made a vertical descent to nestle in among all the engineering equipment.

The engineer released the Huey at noon. There followed a number of routine afternoon missions, dull but important. The Huey had completed its list of missions by 16.00hrs and returned to home base. The day seemed over. But as the first helicopter back our Huey was the first available for anything else dreamed up by the brass during the day. Something had been.

It was decided that an urgent message had to reach

all inhabitants of a nearby village. In a matter of minutes the Huey had a public address system installed. It took off and circled the village for the next hour, with a Vietnamese broadcasting the message. This did complete the day's missions.

After inspection and tender loving care from the crew chief, the Huey was settled into its revetment. Then a call came. A long range patrol, whose mission was intelligence gathering, was in heavy contact with the enemy. Helicopters were required to snatch the patrol from the VC before being wiped out. This Huey, three other slicks and four gunships were despatched to find it, deep in the jungle and make a night pick up.

Contact was made with the stranded patrol leader by homing on his radio signal and finally identifying him by his strobe light. He briefed the helicopters on the pick-up zone, and while the gunships kept the enemy more than well occupied, the slicks descended into a very black LZ and picked up the first members of the patrol. The other slicks followed and soon all were safely aboard. For this particular Huey crew, it really was the end of the day.

Below:
Every soldier in Vietnam appreciated the 'Dust off' lifeline — the airborne medical teams which saved thousands of wounded men's lives. This is a typical end of mission scene for a Huey medevac sortie. *Bell*

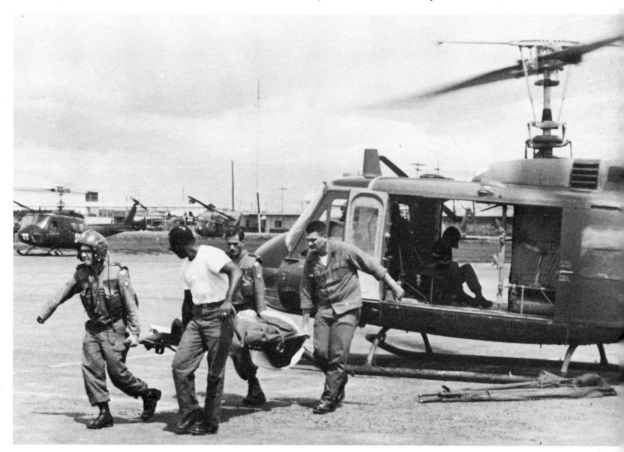

4. Marine Hueys

By late 1964, having had ample demonstration of the UH-1's capabilities as a gunship, and experienced some disappointment with stop-gap armed UH-34s, the Marine Corps placed an order worth over $7million for its own version, the UH-1E. The UH-1 had

been declared the winner of the Corps' ASH — assault support helicopter — competition on 3 March 1962, and that October a replacement programme was initiated to bring VMO squadrons up to strength and to replace both the O-1 and OH-43 with the UH-1 on a one-to-one basis. On 6 January 1963 Bell received an order for an initial batch of 72 UH-1Es (out of an eventual total of 209), plus four examples for testing modifications made to the UH-1B from which the Marines' model was derived.

In order to conduct some evaluation flying before the first UH-1Es were delivered, the Marines borrowed a small number of UH-1Bs from the Army. One of these machines was readied for a flight test by Col Marion E. Carl, Corps Director of Aviation and what ensued served to show the reliability of the Huey, albeit in an unconventional way. A few days before the test was due to take place at Paxutent River, a truck had backed into the elevator of the only available UH-1 and damaged it beyond repair. There was no time to order a replacement, so an elevator was borrowed from an Army UH-1A at nearby Fort

Belvoir. The only problem was that the elevators of the A and B models were of a different size. Learning of the problem, Col Carl showed no dismay and duly lifted off, with Marine Capt David A. Spurlock, a test pilot attached to NATC, at the controls. The Huey headed for Washington in low cloud and rain. The anxious eyes that followed the receding Huey needn't have worried, as the machine arrived safely at the Pentagon and proceeded to take up the Deputy Chief of Staff for Research & Development for a look at clearer weather above the overcast. This flight did have an important purpose, as there were some doubts

Below left:
A view well illustrating the need for a rotor brake for UH-1s likely to spend time aboard ship. These Echo models are from HML-367. *USMC*

Below:
Nice airborne view of a Marine Corps UH-1E shows the bulbous fairing over the roof-mounted hoist mechanism standardised upon after the first batch. *Mike Hooks*

as to the visibility from the Huey's cockpit, but after this test no further criticism was voiced.

First and foremost among the new features on the UH-1E was a rotor brake, essential for stopping the blades turning on the crowded deck of an assault ship and for preventing them from moving in the wind when such a vessel was underway. The brake was a simple enough disc fitted to the main transmission and hydraulically activated from the cockpit. Radios compatible with air and ground forces' channels had also to be installed, together with an associated wiring change from Army direct current type to Navy-Marine Corps alternating current. The other important difference with the UH-1E was its aluminium construction.

Other helicopters, including the earlier models of the Huey, had been constructed of magnesium. Lighter than aluminium, this material increased payload, a factor that overrode the tendency to corrode and to burn virtually uncontrollably. But the corrosion problem would have been particularly serious in a seagoing environment and the Marines gladly accepted

the slight weight increase of aluminium — which was in any case nullified by the UH-1E's good power reserve.

By January 1963 the first UH-1E was ready for customer inspection and by 30 July Bell had completed all necessary avionics and structural testing. In August the Huey began an evaluation programme by the Board of Inspection & Survey, concluding with carrier qualifications on board the USS *Guadalcanal* in December. Ceremonies at the Bell plant on 21 February 1964 marked the delivery of the first UH-1E (BuAer No 151266) to Marine tactical squadron VMO-1. By that time the USMC order had risen to 100 machines, an investment of nearly $15million.

Nearly eight months later the question of arming Marine UH-1Es arose again, as the situation in Vietnam took on a new urgency; in August 1964 Congress had adopted the Tonkin Gulf Resolution setting the seal on massive US involvement in the fighting. Extensive training with the UH-1E by the VMO squadrons had recognised the lack of an armed helicopter escort and accordingly on 19 September the Chief of Naval Operations (CNO) wrote to the Bureau of Weapons stating the urgent requirement for six ground fire suppression armament kits for the UH-1E to be installed 'within 60 to 90 days'. In order not to

again stir up the muddy waters of the helicopters versus fixed wing close air support argument, the CNO made no mention of the attack role. Instead he stressed that the armament was required for self defence, stating that '...these helicopters perform observation, reconnaissance, and rescue missions forward of friendly lines without armed escort. There is no present system of self defense against ground fire for these helicopters'. The request went through channels and duly ended up with HMX-1 at Quantico which would be responsible for the design of the sub-system. Known as TK-1 (Temporary Kit-1) such a system had recently been developed by HMX-1 for the UH-34 and it was relatively easy to adapt this to the TK-2 system for the Huey.

Similar to the armament of Army gunships, the TK-2 utilised two platforms attached to the common pick-up points of the UH-1s for the Army. On to these platforms, the Marines mounted two M-60C machine guns with a bomb rack bolted below the guns. A normal load for the racks was a 2.75in rocket pod. For weapons aiming a 'ring and post'-type sight was provided in preference to more sophisticated sights which would have meant cockpit modifications. The sight swung up to the top of the cockpit when not in use, the forward point of it being a small piece of black tape on the windscreen.

The TK-2 kits were test-fired at NAS Patuxent River with few problems apart from a slight risk of ejected cartridge links from the left hand guns striking the tail rotor. The guns were slightly repositioned and

Below:
Armed UH-1E, BuAer No 151267/UV-20.

deflector plates were subsequently fitted. The need for the armed Hueys to be deployed operationally meant however, that the damage risk to the tail rotor had initially to be accepted, the deflector plates requiring time to fit.

The completed kits were sent to VMO-6 at Camp Pendleton on 15 January 1965 and by 31 March, so successful had they proved that 33 more were requested. Other armaments were also tested during the period, including two GE .50cal SM-14 machine gun pods. These were found to have greater effective range than the 7.62cal M-60s, although their added weight restricted their use to special missions only. The other successful gun mounting was an Emerson TAT-101 nose turret. Containing two M-60s and aimed and controlled by the pilot, these turrets were installed on UH-1Es beginning April 1967, 94 kits being purchased. They were discontinued in April 1972, by which time other armament fits had become available.

On 3 May 1965, the Marines introduced armed Hueys to Vietnam when six machines of VMO-2 arrived at Da Nang, nearly two months after the first Marine infantry battalion had landed there. The armed Hueys were quickly used to good effect and on

Below:
On a beach 17 miles south of Chu Lai in October 1967, a UH-1E of VMO-6 prepares to escort the HMM-263 UH34s lifting off behind it. The Huey had the Marines' TK-2 armament kit. *USMC*

11 August 27 UH-1Es of VMO-6 sailed from Long Beach as part of a major build-up of US Marine forces in the war zone. Increasing congestion at Da Nang forced a move to one of a number of new helicopter bases then being built, Marine Air Group 16, of which the VMO squadrons were part, being relocated at Marble Mountain by 26 August. Marble Mountain lay a few miles east of Da Nang and had a 2,000ft runway of Marston matting. It was a pleasant enough spot in a country where the climate invariably hampered air and associated ground-support operations in numerous ways. Aircraft maintenance became something of a nightmare on bases where there was no hangarage available. Ground crews alternately sweltered in the heat of the summer and sheltered from cold downpours during the monsoon season. Many items were in short supply in the early days and the situation was aggravated by helicopter procurement programmes which had anticipated flying hours far below those that were actually clocked up in the combat zone. Rotor blades were a particular problem; sandblasted by the fine dust that abounded at the bases, they had constantly to be changed when the metal surfaces eroded in the dust storms created by every take-off. By the end of August some UH-1Es had, in common with other Marine helicopter types, to be grounded for lack of replacement rotor blades. The Huey's blades were normally expected to last for 1,000 flight hours, but Vietnam conditions brought this down to 200 hours. The supply of blades was speeded up, although the Huey's other problem, of the ejected cartridges

causing tail damage, persisted. Then on 27 October, disaster struck.

That night, the Viet Cong launched a well planned and co-ordinated attack on Marble Mountain. By surprising the Marine personnel, the enemy was able to systematically destroy 19 helicopters and heavily damage 11. Thirteen of the casualties were MAG-16's UH-1Es and with two more Hueys badly damaged and another pair suffering minor damage, the unit was reduced to just four flyable aircraft.

Despite this setback, MAG-16 was able to fly an impressive 333 individual sorties, assisted by helicopters loaned by other units. But more UH-1s were urgently requested for Vietnam. There were only 18 Hueys — other than those in SE Asia — in the entire Marine Corps, and two of these were in the Caribbean. By November, 12 aircraft had arrived; three of these had the 540 rotor system — although the Corps then lacked any spares for these otherwise improved Hueys, and the Army was asked to help out. Also critical was the loss of the TK-2 armament packages and it was December before more kits reached the combat units.

There followed a period of making do for the Marine VMO squadrons equipped with UH-1s. By carefully marshalling its resources, the Corps was able to meet its helicopter commitment; the grinding war of attrition in Vietnam demanded staggeringly-high numbers of men and machines — and placed a very great operational utilisation on those aircraft assigned

Below:
The first Marine Corps UH-1Es had a TAT-101 nose turret containing two M-60 machine guns. *Peter Newark*

to the combat squadrons. Two new VMO squadrons were authorised in mid-1966, although these did not instantly bring about additional capability in Vietnam. One unit had to be retained for training the additional pilots the Corps needed. By March 1966 the Marines had 58 UH-1Es in active units, although it was authorised 76, and moves were made to loan 20 UH-1Bs from the Army.

These Hueys were transferred in two lots, 10 in August 1966 and 10 the following January. Assigned to training duties, thus releasing UH-1Es for combat use, these B models were unmodified and were therefore of limited value to the Marines, particularly for shipboard training, because they lacked rotor brakes. Nevertheless the Corps was glad to have them.

Budget constraints for Fiscal Year 1966 trimmed the Marines' request for 108 additional UH-1Es to 59, 31 for the new VMO squadrons. None were approved for use by the reserves. Desperate to boost this meagre number, the Corps suggested transferring funds from other programmes to get the additional Hueys and in July 1967, approval was given for ordering 27 more. At the same time, VMO-3 was activated as the first of the two new 'add on' squadrons. With 12 UH-1Es, the first detachment of VMO-3 left for Vietnam on 9 December. On 17 December VMO-5 was formed for training UH-1E crews, a task it continued to undertake until March 1968.

The UH-1E continues to serve the Marines in the 1980s, there being six utility squadrons with a mix of Echo models and UN-1Ns to support the three active Marine Air Wings. In addition, the Marine Corps Air Reserve Force, controlled by the 4th MAW, currently has two squadrons of UH-1Es.

5.
Navy Hueys

The US Navy became a Huey helicopter operator in the mid-1960s as a result of its Vietnam commitment to keeping the waterways of the Mekong Delta open and free from enemy interference. This duty fell to Task Force 116, codenamed 'Game Warden', established in December 1965 to employ various types of small boat transport including armed patrol boats (PBRs) and hovercraft — some of which were also made by Bell. These vessels occasionally met with heavy opposition along the river banks of the Delta and it was proposed that helicopters be employed to support and protect them. The Navy however, lacked both helicopters and trained crews to carry out this mission, despite having been the procurement service for the Marine Corps' UH-1E programme, and so it turned to the Army to provide initial equipment. A request was passed to the pioneer Army Huey unit in Vietnam, the 197th Aviation Company (334th Aviation Company from September 1966) for the loan of eight UH-1Bs. The agreement did not cover crews, as the Navy provided these from Helicopter Support Squadron One (HC-1) at NAS Ream Field, California, a unit previously experienced in operating detachments from carriers mainly on SAR work.

Four detachments were formed, each consisting of eight pilots, eight crewmen and two UH-1Bs. The first, Detachment 29, arrived at Vung Tau early in July for theatre training under the auspices of the Army. Five weeks were spent on familiarisation with the Huey's systems and armament together with studies of the tactics of patrol boat support. On 14 August Cdr William A. Rockwell took Detachment 29 aboard the USS *Tortuga* (LSD-26) and on 19 September Naval aviators prepared to fly attack helicopters in combat for the first time when the unit officially took over the role of River Patrol Force support. Headquarters was established at Vung Tau and the three other detachments were installed at Nha Be in the Rung Sat special zone, at Vinh Long, and aboard a second dock landing

ship, USS *Comstock* (LSD-19). By the time the Navy had used its armed helicopters in action, the Army had given the unit (known, since its arrival in Vietnam, as HC-1 Detachment Vung Tau) the nickname 'Seawolves'. Having just the right ring to it, the name stuck.

The first operation took place on 31 October, Navy gunships going after a group of sampans that had been spotted by the PBRs. In three hours, the helicopters destroyed 50 out of a force of 75 and inflicted many casualties among the troops the sampans were carrying.

On 11 November the first of the specially-configured tank landing ships (LSTs) arrived to replace the USS *Comstock*. The new ship had the facilities to support two UH-1Bs and a squadron of 10 PBRs, including quarters for helicopter crews, JP5 fuel stowage, ammunition stores and night landing light systems. There were four LSTs in all, three of which were engaged on operational support with one on maintenance duty at all times between 1967 and 1968 and with one vessel on maintenance availability. They were stationed along the lower Bassac, Co Chien and Ham Luong Rivers in the Delta and moved around periodically to be near trouble spots and as a security measure.

After further actions, the detachments changed numbers when they became detachments of Helicopter Attack (Light) Squadron Three (HA(L)-3) early in 1967, the squadron being officially commissioned on 1 April at Vung Tau. There were then 32 officers, 32 enlisted men and eight UH-1Bs, but by August the helicopter complement was boosted by further Hueys passed on by the 1st Cavalry Division. Until the end of the year, HA(L)-3 was continually engaged in support operations, flown in the face of considerable maintenance difficulties which stemmed from having to rely on Army chains of command. By December there were seven detachments consisting of a total of 22 helicopters using land bases as well as three LSTs.

The undoubted value of the Seawolves' helicopters in the counter-insurgency effort led to the establishment of a crew training programme in 1967. It included an intensive 16-day transition course on the UH-1B at Fort Rucker's Rotary Wing Training Department and a maintenance and gunnery course for the enlisted personnel. The latter course was devised by the Door Gunner Training Branch, Aviation Armament Division, Department of Tactics — which also worked with the pilots on the ranges using the XM-16 and XM-21 gun systems and 2.75in rockets. The courses were comprehensive, covering all aspects of river convoy escort, fire support, low level navigation, support of SEAL — SEa Air Land commandos — operations and the use of Firefly night searchlights.

By the end of 1967, the Seawolves had turned in an impressive record; since commissioning the squadron had flown over 7,000 missions and 9,744 hours on a variety of operations including assisting beleaguered outposts covering downed aircraft and medevac as well as its primary task of riverine support. The Navy Hueys quickly built a fine reputation for getting the job done and their night-flying capability was greatly appreciated because it meant that river patrols had protection around the clock. Night patrols put another 200-300 hours in the log books of helicopter pilots already flying more than 600 hours per tour during daylight.

A typical night patrol from Vinh Long took the form of an early sunset briefing on known VC activity areas. A two-ship Huey element formed lead and trail elements, the lead flying at about 500ft with rotating beacon and navigation lights burning. The trail Huey kept station at higher altitude, blacked out. If the lead ship was fired on, the trail Huey would drop down and engage, surprising the enemy concentrating on the 'illuminated' lead helicopter.

During the hectic activity of the 1968 Tet offensive, the Seawolves were instrumental in helping PBRs and SEALs prevent the city of Chau Loc being overrun by the enemy, and at Ben Tre the same team fought a 36hr running battle with the same successful con-clusion. Some of the enemy did manage to get into Vinh Long City, home of Detachment 3, but a concerted effort by the helicopters and boats repulsed them after a series of operations, some of which involved evacuations.

Throughout 1968 Game Warden forces continued operations and moved nearer the Cambodian border in an effort to stop supplies for the VC reaching Vietnam. Late in the year came Operation 'Giant Sling', so named because the area of operations, between the Vam Co Tay and Vam Co Dong Rivers in the Parrot's Beak area, was shaped like a huge slingshot in the countryside.

By the early part of 1969 a new HQ and maintenance base for HA(L)-3 was ready, and the unit moved to it from Vung Tau in the spring. Release of more Army UH-1B and C models in favour of the new HueyCobra meant that the Navy squadron could boost its Huey complement from 22 to 33. Along with increased numbers of aircraft, new duties were allocated to it and the Seawolves' helicopters carried mail, passengers and freight on numerous liaison flights undertaken by a separate detachment known as

Below:
Seawolves' lair. A Navy UH-1 departs its support vessel off the Vietnam coast. *Bell*

Above:
An HH-1K assigned to NAS Jacksonville, Florida, in July 1970. *George Pennick*

the 'Sealords'. Equipped with four UH-1Ls, only eight of which had been procured by the Navy, the Sealords were established at Binh Thuy in November 1969, two UH-1Cs also being assigned that month.

A utility and training version of the Huey, the UH-1L had the uprated Lycoming T-53-L-13 engine offering 1,100shp and was an improved version of the Army UH-1C, having its direct Army equivalent in the UH-1M. The UH-1L was part of a procurement programme for the Huey begun by the Navy in 1968, primarily to fulfil a training role. On 16 May 1968 the service ordered 45 TH-1Ls along with the eight UH-1L utility ships, following selection of the UH-1 as the Navy's advanced rotary-wing trainer. The first UH-1L was accepted on 3 November. A further order for single engined Hueys was placed in 1969 for 27 HH-1Ks for air sea rescue. Also powered by the T-53-L-13 engine, this version was similar to the UH-1E for the Marines, but had improved avionics.

In the meantime, the Navy Hueys continued their frustrating war against the Viet Cong; despite intensive efforts to interdict the supply routes from the North, enemy activity remained constant. There were always areas that the Seawolves could not patrol on a regular basis due to the size of the operational area and limited resources, despite the increased number of helicopters received in 1969. By the end of that year, Game Warden forces reached their peak strength, with approximately 22 boat squadrons and 33 Hueys. The unit still experienced problems in maintaining all available helicopters on virtually a 'round the clock' basis and it should be stressed that although HA(L)-3 was allocated 33 Hueys, this complement was not realised until near the end of its active life. In an effort to boost gunship availability, the UH-1Ls were armed, initially

on an experimental basis. Such was the constant need for gunnery support for river-borne operations that all the L models were subsequently adapted to carry weapons.

By early 1970 six HA(L)-3 detachments were shore-based, with three embarked on LST or YRBM — Repair, Berthing and Messing Barge, Non-Self-Propelled — vessels, and in May these units were part of the US invasion force for Cambodia. Known as Operation 'Tran Hung Dao XI' to Game Warden forces, this controversial thrust into the Viet Cong sanctuaries saw HA(L)-3's Hueys become the first American helicopters to reach the Cambodian capital, Phnom Penh. Five detachments saw action in Cambodia, the three main ones (Nos 8, 9 and 5) logging 748 combat sorties. The seven Sealords' UH-1Ls — one having crashed on 26 April — also flew during the operation and notched up a new Navy flight time record of 961 hours. The value of the 'offshore' bases was proven on the infrequent occasions that the Seawolves' shore bases came under enemy attack. The ships were far less vulnerable to mortar and rocket attack.

By the end of 1970, HA(L)-3 had 35 Bell Iroquois helicopters — 27 UH-1Bs, two UH-1Cs, two HH-1Ks and four UH-1Ls. Operations continued into the following spring, when the first UH-1M was delivered to the squadron. Many of the Mike models had been reconditioned by the Army facility at Corpus Christi, Texas and such was their availability that the Seawolves began to replace their UH-1Bs with M models fairly rapidly, replacing the original -11 engine with the -13 after about 100 hours operation. The result was a vastly superior aircraft with greater range by virtue of its larger fuel tanks offering better on target loiter time, plus the ability to carry the variety of heavy weapons vital to the unit's mission.

By August 1970 the Vietnamisation of the war meant that on most missions the Seawolves' gunships carried an ARVN observer and the first VNAF personnel arrived to learn riverine support operations. These qualified pilots and gunners were to take over the Seawolves' mission as withdrawal of US forces from Vietnam gathered momentum and by early 1972 orders brought HA(L)-3's deactivation nearer. Ceremonies at Binh Thuy on 26 January marked the passing of a successful and unique Navy squadron after five years of operations.

TH-1L and UH-1Ls continue to provide training for Navy helicopter crews, including carrier qualification — which the Navy requires of its helicopter pilots as well as those who fly fixed wing types. In addition to supporting the active duty Air Wings, the UH-1 is an integral part of the Reserve Helicopter Wing which has seven squadrons flying a mix of HH-1s, HH-3s and SH-3Ds.

6.
Squad Carrier

It was because of a need to get more lifting capacity out of the basic UH-1B airframe that Bell developed what might be termed the 'second phase' Huey, the UH-1D. With a 3ft 5in fuselage stretch, the Delta model began life as the YHU-1D under the pre-1962 designation system. There were seven pre-production machines, subsequently designated YUH-1D and UH-1D, with serial numbers 60-6028 to 60-6034. These and approximately two thirds of the production models had the T53-L-11 engine of 1,100shp, the remainder the 1,400shp L-13 (which also powered the majority of the similar UH-1H models). The prototype YHU-1D made its first flight on 16 August 1961.

The fuselage stretch was enough to enable the helicopter to accommodate a full squad of 12 combat troops, with a maximum of 14, and their weapons. The 220sq ft cargo compartment could alternatively accept six stretchers plus three seats for medevac work or various passenger/cargo loads. The number of troops carried by Army UH-1Ds in Vietnam tended to vary according to their nationality. Tests had shown that the fully-equipped Vietnamese soldier averaged 167lb. Ten men at this weight, plus the American crew of four, armour plate, weapons, a tool box, a water container, a case of emergency rations and armoured vests for the crew grossed 8,700lb — or 2,100lb over the UH-1B's normal gross weight and 200lb over its maximum operational weight. The consequence of this had been to limit Huey slicks to eight troops except in a dire emergency. It was also directed that armed helicopters would operate with no more than the normal complement of five personnel and armament. Although the Delta usually carried only two more troops than the B model, it had a far more acceptable safety margin, and in a combat situation where the 'dire emergency' was often the norm one or two extra passengers did not unduly stress the machine. Larger

Below:
In the air ambulance role, the Delta could carry up to six stretchers in various locations in the cabin. The arrangement shown made for ultra-quick loading of battlefield casualties.
Barry Wheeler

cargo doors facilitated loading of personnel and cargo and enabled this to be done from either side simultaneously and thus shorten the time spent in the landing zone. The flat freeboard floor enabled bulky loads to be carried with ease, even when these were wider than the cabin's 8ft 6in. Total payload of the UH-1D was 4,900lb, with maximum take-off weight established as 9,500lb. The higher rated engine gave the aircraft a maximum speed of 120kt, 110kt cruise and a normal range of 253nm, although auxiliary fuel tanks could boost this to more than 600nm. In addition to internal loads, the floor-mounted hook could take up to 4,000lb.

The VH-1D's rotor was similar to that of the F model with 27in chord blades increased in diameter to 48ft, necessitating lengthening the tailboom by 18in to provide clearance for the main blades, which had a characteristic droop. The Delta had a pronounced nose up attitude both in the air and on the ground which distinguished it from other models. But the most reliable recognition feature was the twin cabin windows on each side compared with one on all short-fuselage model Hueys. These, plus a longer transmission housing with twin cooling grilles aft of the rotor mast and the distinctive small door aft of the pilots doors, all helped observers pick out a Delta transport from a B or C model gunship.

Another clue was armament; with the decision to use the smaller UH-1s as gunships, the UH-1D was most widely used in the transportation or medevac roles and it was unusual for it to be armed with anything but a single door-pillar mounted M-60 machine gun on each side, at least in US Army service. With far fewer machines on strength, No 9 Squadron RAAF equipped its UH-1Ds with a formidable gunship kit, ending up with helicopters that were more heavily armed than many of their US counterparts. The Vietnamese also outfitted their UH-1Ds and Hs with heavy armament, it being common for aircraft operated later in the war and after the US withdrawal to have door mounted miniguns in place of the M-60s.

Seven months after the first flight of the YUH-1D, Bell claimed the first of a series of record flights for the new sub-type. Three Army pilots flew the aircraft in these record flights, which began on 13 April 1962 when Capt Boyce B. Buckner cpatured the time to climb to a given altitude record. (Further details of this and all other UH-1 records are given in the appendix section of this book.)

The Army accepted the first UH-1D on 31 May 1963 and the type was issued to field units from 9 August. By late the following year some 375 were in Vietnam, and by mid-1965 about 30 were reaching the war zone every month. The 11th Air Assault Division (forerunner of the 1st Cav Divn) at Fort Benning was the first recipient of the Delta, its deliveries including

the second and third production machines, s/n 62-2107 and 62-2108. The US Army eventually accepted a total of 2,008 UH-1Ds, production running to 2,561 and including foreign orders, pre-production machines and HH-1D conversions to the rescue role. Also included were 10 aircraft for the Canadian Armed Forces initially designated CUH-1D but which became CUH-1H with the more powerful T53-L-13.

During the decade that the single-engined Hueys were establishing themselves with the US Army, Navy and Marines, Bell continued development work and concurrently met unprecedentedly high orders. The early 1960s also saw the start of a flood of production orders from other nations for what was to become one of the most widely used series of helicopters in the world.

Some idea of the value of the 'Vietnam war programme' to Bell can be noted by quoting some figures. On 29 October 1963 the company received a contract for UH-1B and D models valued at more than $108million; 24 December 1964 was the day a contract was placed for 720 B/D models worth $98million; and approval of 405 UH-1Ds for West Germany on 5 April 1965 was worth $125million. Just over a year later, Bell was able to record the largest contract in its history and the largest ever awarded by US Army Aviation Material Command. Covering no less than 2,115 UH-1s, it was valued at $249,457,443.

From 1960 Bell Helicopter was an operating division of Textron Incorporated, the Providence, Rhode Island concern having purchased the defence activities of Bell Aircraft Corporation on 5 July. Thenceforward Bell Aerospace had three divisions: Bell Helicopter, Bell Aerosystems Co, and Hydraulic Research & Manufacturing Co.

After the death of Larry Bell in 1956, E. J. Ducayet became President of Bell Helicopter. Honoured with the Presidency of the American Helicopter Society, Ducayet remained at the head of Bell until December 1971 when he became Chairman. James F. Atkins then took over as President of Bell Helicopter.

The fourth and last US service to equip with the UH-1 was the Air Force, which announced a new version based on the B model as the winner of a selective competition on 7 June 1963. The choice was undoubtedly influenced by Bell's agreement to adapt the UH-1B airframe to take a General Electric T58 engine, plentiful stocks of which were held by the Air Force at that time. The powerplant was the same as that used in the Sikorsky HH-3/S-61 series and potentially offered some economies, particularly on servicing costs. Even so, considerable engineering

Left:
The standard armament of a UH-1D 'slick' in Vietnam was the trusty M-60 machine gun, one being mounted on each side and stowed in the manner shown. *US Army*

Top:
UH-1Ds of the 229th Assault Helicopter Battalion prepare to lift off for the combat landing zone. Machines of A, B and C Companies were identified by blue triangle, square and circle markings respectively. *Bell*

Above:
The second YUH-1D (60-6029) flew another series of Huey flight records in 1962. *via Barry Wheeler*

Right:
Maj E. F. Sampson was one of the Army pilots who flew the record-breaking YUH-1D. *Bruce Robertson*

Top left:
An attractive silver and yellow tail band finish is carried by Brazilian Air Force UH-1Ds employed in the rescue role. *Bell*

Centre left:
The UH-1F was unique to the USAF. The first of 120 delivered is seen here on flight test. *Mike Hooks*

Bottom left:
With minigun door armament and typical SE Asian USAF camouflage, 63-13139 was part of the first batch of Foxtrot models for the USAF. *Bell*

Above:
A third batch machine, this F model has the early USAF dark blue and white paint scheme.

changes were necessary to adapt it to UH-1 installation. Unlike the Lycoming engine, which had its driveshaft running forward to the main transmission, the GE unit ran its driveshaft aft, and exhausted through a side-mounted pipe. This meant that in the UH-1 it had to be mounted backwards, with the rear end of the original T53 exhaust pipe blanked off and a new one cut in the side of the transmission housing (which was entirely redesigned) on the starboard side.

The first UH-1F (first designated XH-48A under the USAF aircraft nomenclature system) flew on 20 February 1964 as s/n 63-13141; the first operational F model was delivered on 23 September 1964 and went to the 4486th Test Squadron at Eglin AFB later that month. The initial order was for 25 machines, with subsequent contracts meeting the balance of 95 by 1967. Deliveries totalled 120 in standard form and there were 26 similar TH-1Fs configured as instrument trainers. The 540 rotor system was fitted, giving the UH-1F a maximum cruising speed of 120kt at a maximum gross weight of 9,000lb. Air Force UH-1Fs also had a cargo compartment at the front end of the tailboom (which was the same as the boom fitted to the D model) with a door on the starboard side. Up to 4,000lb of cargo could be lifted as an alternative to the full passenger complement of 10, and some TH-1F instrument trainers were also used for hoist training, although this equipment was not fitted to Air Force F models.

The USAF ordered the Huey primarily for support of its Minuteman and Titan missile silos dispersed throughout the midwestern US, with the additional capability of performing a base rescue mission, mainly with Military Airlift Command's Aerospace Rescue & Recovery Service. Air Force Hueys were also used on general utility duties, including support for TAC fighter wings and crew training units.

A Huey version unique to the USAF was the UH-1P; 20 F models were converted, the designation referring to equipment installed for the psychological warfare mission. The majority of UH-1Ps were issued to squadrons of the 1st Special Operations Wing at Hurlburt Field, Florida, among them the 7th SOW and 549th Special Operations Training Squadron (TASTS).

43

Above:
Vietnamese troops loading one of the SVNAF's UH-1H models. *Barry Wheeler*

Right:
Pilot's seat details seen to advantage on 68-15556, a UH-1H of the 173rd Aviation Company at Aldershot, UK in June 1973. *R. L. Ward*

Some were deployed to Vietnam during the late 1960s and subsequently used on regular air base and unit support in company with UH-1Fs after their return to the US. By the early 1980s the Air Force had generally replaced its F/P models with the UH-1N and passed some of the former to agencies such as the US Department of Forestry, while others went into storage at MASDC.

Substitution of the Lycoming T53-L-13 in the UH-1D airframe produced the UH-1H, which became the standard US Army transport in the latter half of the 1960s and throughout the 1970s. Externally identical to the Delta model, the UH-1H superseded the former in production, and many UH-1Ds were brought up to H standard. Bell received a $2,700 million contract for the design, production and testing of two YUH-1H prototypes on 4 April 1966, and delivered the first examples to the US Army in September 1967.

Bell produced a total of 5,435 H models, the majority of which went to the US Army, although the type was widely used by foreign air arms, including Vietnam. New Zealand was the first actual customer with an order for nine aircraft (those for Vietnam and

Starboard side view of '556 reveals the extensive plumbing of the T53 engine. *R. L. Ward*

Port side view of '556 shows how the engine panels fold back for ease of maintenance. *R. L. Ward*

Cambodia being transferred from US Army stocks) and Nationalist China ordered 118 for Army use under an agreement signed on 19 August 1969 whereby the Aero Industry Development Centre at Taichung built the Model 205 under license. In the event, the initial order was modified drastically, to less than 30 machines and was followed by a second contract for 24, announced by Bell on 2 August 1972. Under the agreement, Bell supplied the Chinese factory — owned and operated by the Chinese Nationalist Air Force — with components for

assembly, the resulting helicopters incorporating a number of locally-made parts. The follow-on contract included an agreement for Bell to supply tooling for production of main and tail rotor blades, and other items.

Other early UH-1H customers were Canada, which ordered 10 examples for the CAF's Mobile Command under the designation CH-118, and the USAF for 30 HH-1Hs intended for local base rescue duties. The Canadian machines, known to Bell as CUH-1Hs, were delivered from 6 March 1968.

UH-1H of a US Army Airevac detachment at Landsthul, Germany in September 1974. *George Pennick*

Above:
A special version of the UH-1C became the Mike model when fitted with the INFANT — Iroquois Night Fighter and Night Tracker — system. Designed to deny the enemy the cover of darkness, it employed low light level TV tracking. *US Army*

Unusual Designations

Although modifications to the basic UH-1H airframe resulted in the prefix letter designators HH-1H and EH-1H, the latter identifying conversions to electronic warfare duties under the US Army Security Agency's Project Quick Fix, one other suffix letter has been used, for the UH-1V. This, together with the intervening B/C model derivatives, the twins and the Cobras, means that there has been a Huey sub-type using nearly every letter of the alphabet. While the J suffix was taken up by the SeaCobra, the Army's SOTAS — Stand Off Target Acquisition System — programme produced the JUH-1.

Funded in 1975, the heart of SOTAS was an elongated radar pod intended for use on the Sikorsky EH-60 Black Hawk. Part of the test programme involved four UH-1Hs (two of them were Nos 63-12974 and 63-12976) configured with rectractable skids enabling the pod to be slung from the belly of each machine to provide adequate ground clearance and to enable the pod to rotate whilst in flight. The cross tubes were extended to give the necessary clearance on the ground and each JUH-1 carried additional sensor equipment in the nose compartment. Half the passenger/cargo compartment was occupied by the transceiver equipment and a new autopilot and navigation system was installed. Two JUH-1s deployed to Germany in 1975 for flight tests in conjunction with a DME/localiser and data link to a ground station equipped with inter-active CRT displays. By 1979, two units of two aircraft were assigned to Germany, tests continuing until at least 1980.

And the UH-1V? This is the unofficial designation given to UH-1Hs modified by the Army Electronics Command at Lakehurst, New Jersey. Equipment includes a radio altimeter, DME, glide slope and a hoist, the aircraft so designated being employed in the medevac role. The first unit to get the UH-1V was the 397th Aeromedical Detachment, New Hampshire Army National Guard, at Concord, New Hampshire.

It remains to be seen if there will be a UH-1W; the letters X and Y almost certainly will not be allocated. Leaving only Z, which if the longevity of the Huey continues, just might be.

The Iranian 'Isfahan'

Development of the single-engined UH-1 series was substantially boosted in 1972 by an order from Iran for a new model tailored specifically to operation in the 'hot and high' conditions prevailing in that part of the world. This was the Model 214A, 287 examples of which were ordered by the Shah's regime along with 202 AH-1J Cobras. The contract was placed on 22 December 1972 by the US Army, acting on Iran's behalf with initial funding of $28.5million. Total value of the order was $500million.

Ten years or so before the fervour of Islam eliminated one of America's biggest customers for military equipment, Bell had begun negotiations that were to lead to the founding of a separate division of Textron Inc solely to do business with Iran. Maj-Gen Delk M. Oden, US Army retired, was named President

Above:
The first of Iran's Model 214As, 6-4651. *Bell*

of the new concern in March 1973. Whereas early Iranian orders were placed through the US Government, establishment of the Textron subsidiary was one of the first steps towards providing Iran with a modern aerospace industry, starting with the manufacture of helicopters. Bell was named as Iran's joint partner on 21 November 1975. With co-production of the Model 214A underway, it was intended that 400 examples would be built in Iran and to that end a factory and training complex was planned at Isfahan, some 250 miles from Tehran.

Bell flew a demonstrator 214 prototype for the first time in October 1970, from the Arlington test facility. The new machine, known as the Model 214 Huey-Plus, was a strengthened UH-1H airframe married to a single 1,900shp Lycoming T53-L-702 engine. It had the transmission drive system developed for the experimental KingCobra and the larger, 50ft diameter rotor that reduced noise, offered better performance at high speeds and enabled the 214 to operate at weights approximately half as much again as the 5,000lb payload of the UH-1H.

Bell built three additional 214 prototypes before moving on to the production version for Iran, the Model 214A. A prototype powered by a 2,050shp T55-L-7C was shipped to Iran in August 1972 for evaluation by the Shah's military advisors and as a result of these trials, Bell increased performance even further in production 214A models, by substituting the 2,930shp Lycoming LTC4B-8D. This engine enable operation at a gross weight of 16,000lb, carrying up to 15 troops or an external payload of 7,500lb.

The first prototype 214A (N214J) flew for the first time on 13 March 1974, the second and third machines following in April and May respectively. These three prototypes completed all necessary trials and certifica-

tion work in the next 12 months or so and in March 1975 Bell completed the first example of the Iranian order for 287. Deliveries officially began on 26 April, and on the 29th the first production aircraft (c/n 27004, IIA serial 6-4651) was flown to five new world records in Iran. In the hands of Manouchehr Khosrowdad, Commanding General of the Imperial Iranian Army Aviation, the new 'Isfahan' helicopter achieved maximum sustained altitude; time to climb and horizontal flight marks. The flights were made with Clem Bailey, assistant chief production test pilot for Textron, as co-pilot. By August 1975, Bell was producing nine Isfahans a month and output peaked at 20 per month in February 1977, the last 214A of the original order being completed on 19 December that year. Six more ordered in March 1977 were completed by the autumn of 1978.

While the Isfahans were entering service in the trooping and heavy-lift transport roles with the Iranian Army, Bell received a further order for 39 similar machines from the Imperial Iranian Air Force. These aircraft, configured for the air-sea rescue role, were ordered in February 1976; first flown that October as the Model 214C, deliveries commenced in January 1977 and were completed in March 1978 with hand over of the final two.

As with the majority of UH-1 models, Bell offered a civil counterpart to the Model 214 as the 214B BigLifter. Differing only in detail to its military counterpart, it found a relatively small civilian market. Only 70 were built, five of which were purchased by the Government of Oman for utility duties and delivered in 1975.

7.
Twin Turbos

Despite the impressive performance of the Model 533 in compound configuration, this did not lead to production of the UH-1 in any radical form. Instead, Bell turned to a simpler solution to give the Huey more power and the increased safety factor of twin engines.

Having opened new engineering and research facilities at Fort Worth in February 1964, the company funded the first twin conversion itself and planned a spring 1965 completion date for it. A UH-1D served as the prototype Model 208 Twin

Below:
South American countries have been good Huey customers. This red, white and silver example is one of the Peruvian Air Force's Bell 212s.

Delta, the first flight being made on 29 April 1965. Incorporating a Continental XT67-T-1 free turbine comprising two T72-T-2 Model 217, turboshafts coupled to a common reduction gearbox and output shaft, the new powerplant offered 1,200shp flat rated to 1,240shp for take-off and 1,100shp in continuous flight. A rotor brake was fitted as standard.

Bell's growth programme for the Huey was aimed to a considerable extent at the civil market, where the additional safety factor of a second engine made it attractive, particularly in off-shore oil and gas exploration support work and rescue operations. Civil versions of the single-engined models, most notably the Model 205, had aroused market interest, but it was the developed Model 208, the Model 212 'Twin Two Twelve', that was to become the most popular.

Initial military interest in the 212 was from Canada, the result of an understanding with Bell that the aircraft would be powered by engines built by United Aircraft of Canada. Generally similar to the UH-1D (apart from the larger engine cowling incorporating two intakes abreast of the main rotor mast and twin exhausts), the first production Model 212 made its maiden flight in April 1969. The Canadians duly ordered 50 initially designed CUH-1H (subsequently CH-135) following their government's approval for development to proceed on the basis of using UAC/Pratt & Whitney PT6T-3 engines. The 'Turbo Twin Pack', as this powerplant was called, offered a performance similar to that of the coupled Continental units, giving the 212 a cruising speed of 121mph and a range of 312 miles at a loaded weight of 10,000lb.

UH-1A 57-6102 of the US Army Aviation Board.
Mike Hooks

The official hand-over of the first CUH-1N was at Uplands Airport, Ottawa, on 3 May 1971, the full order being completed a year later. The CH-135 progressively replaced the CH-118 in CAF service and was used on similar liaison, utility and base rescue duties.

Even before the Canadian order had been officially confirmed, the USAF, Navy and Marines had placed orders for the new twin under the military designation UH-1N. The first buy was respectively 79, 40 and 22 for the three US services, basic equipment being similar. Up to 14 passengers could be accommodated and there was provision for an external load of 3,385lb. Optional equipment included a cargo sling, rescue hoist, emergency flotation and high skid gear.

The USAF formerly accepted the UH-1N on 2 October 1970 at a ceremony at Eglin AFB; service deployment of the initial 79 machines included units of TAC, MAC, USAFE, Southern and Pacific Command and Air Force Headquarters. Twenty two examples used in the rescue role were identified as HH-1Ns, while VIP transports, used primarily by the 89th MAW (later MAG) at Andrews AFB were VH-1Ns. The majority of HH-1Ns served with the Air Force Reserve and 10 went to the Special Operations Force, the USAF's counter-insurgency, anti-terrorist unit based at Hurlburt Field.

The Navy role for the UH-1N was also primarily that of base rescue at air stations and the type was also employed on support duties in the annual Operation 'Deep Freeze' exercise in the Antarctic. Serving with Antarctic Development Squadron Six (VXE-6) at

Above:
Highly-polished khaki and white UH-1N of Detachment 2, Aerospace Rescue & Recovery Service, based at Ramstein AB, Germany. *George Pennick*

Below:
In military guise, the UH-1N was a true inter-service helicopter. This is one of the early examples for the US Navy. *Mike Hooks*

NAS North Island, one UH-1N carried parachute
rigger Hendrick V. Gorick to an altitude of 20,500ft
over McMurdo Sound on 6 March 1972. Gorick's
jump set a record for the Antarctic continent.

The total Navy and Marines order for the N model
was 204; six USMC units were equipped with it and
the total included six VH-1N executive transports. The
Marines took delivery of the first November model on
7 April 1971 at New River, Connecticut, the type's
initial assignment being (along with the first Marine
AH-1J SeaCobras) to HMA-269. At that time the unit
was merely an 'activation cadre' pending transfer of
HML-167 from Vietnam. This move was made on
10 June, and on the 28th HML-167 was declared
operational as the first Twin Huey squadron in the
Marine Corps. During a time of significant change in
the complement and deployment of Marine helicopter
squadrons after Vietnam, the Twin Hueys were
destined to spend much of their operational life at sea
aboard a new generation of amphibious assault ships,
able to carry complete combat teams close inshore for
rapid deployment by helicopter, covered if necessary
by their own helicopter gunships. The LPHs remain an
integral part of Marine deployment around the world,
the latest trouble spot being Lebanon, which saw the
USMC contingent of the multi-national peace-keeping
force under fire for the first time since Vietnam.

Further orders for UH-1Ns for the Navy and
Marines were placed during the period 1973-78, the
US Army having previously become the fourth US
service customer for this model with an initial batch of
15 machines.

The Model 214ST

It was to meet a future Iranian requirement for
helicopters with increased weight-lifting capability and
improved performance that led Bell to develop the
ultimate derivative of the basic Model 204/205. The
programme began with the single prototype Model
214 Huey Plus and was followed by a Model 214A
converted to twin-engine configuration with a pair of
General Electric T700 turboshafts. Following
successful trials in Iran, this machine provided the
basis for a production model, initially known as the
214 'Stretched Twin' and later, 'Super Transport'. Bell
built three prototypes, two for the civil production
version and one for the military version, powered by
the uprated T700/T1C engine unit of 2,250hp. It was
intended that Iran would cover 50% of the launch
costs, but when that market was eliminated in the
summer of 1979, only part of these costs had been
paid.

Bell therefore decided to continue the programme
and self-fund it, and the first flight of the 'Bell version'
took place on 21 July 1979. The 214ST had a cabin
area lengthened by about 8ft by inserts ahead of and
behind the main rotor housing. A five-bladed rotor
with 33in chord blades was fitted, the rotor diameter
being 52ft, the largest of any UH-1 derivative. The
Noda-Matic nodalised rotor head suspension system
was fitted and the tail rotor blades were of 14in chord.
For the first time a wheeled version was offered, all
previous models having been supplied with pick-up
points for wheels to 'lift' the skids clear of the ground
for manoeuvring.

Production model 214STs are powered by 2,930shp
Lycoming LTC4B-8D units. Primarily intended for
the civilian market, the 214ST has to date found only
one military customer, that of Venezuala. Two
examples were delivered in the spring of 1982 for the
Air Force.

Above:
UH-1B A2-720 of No 9 Squadron, one of 13 Bravo models used for training by the Royal Australian Air Force.
Eric Allen

Below:
Venezuelan Air Force UH-1Hs on a flight test from Bell's Fort Worth plant. *Bell*

Below:
The first TH-1L for the US Navy was BuAer No 157806. Specifically for training, these machines had the distinctive US Navy training finish of orange and white with black detail. *Bell*

Bottom:
To enable the company to meet the needs of the European and Middle Eastern helicopter market more easily, Bell licensed Agusta of Italy to build the Model 204. This Italian Air Force AB204 is painted in SAR colours. *R. L. Ward*

8.
The Italian Connection

Moves towards establishing a European production line for the UH-1 began in the late 1950s, Bell logically enough favouring Costruzioni Aeronautiche Giovanni Agusta of Italy, which was then building the Model 47 under an agreement signed in 1952. Under the terms of the license, Agusta became the exclusive agency for Bell helicopters throughout the European continent, the Mediterranean and Middle Eastern countries. This lucrative market was then in the process of looking for its next generation of military helicopters, with the Italian armed forces a primary customer. Agusta had also collaborated with Bell on indigenous Italian rotorcraft, drawing considerably on American know-how and using components mated with engines developed in Europe. Thus the basis had already been laid for the manufacture of Bell UH-1 models powered either by US or European engines.

At that time, the major manufacturers of helicopter powerplants in Western Europe were British and French. Britain's Bristol Siddeley led the field with turboshafts such as the Nimbus, Gnome and Coupled Gnome, and it was to be the Gnome, a UK version of the General Electric T58, that was chosen to power the Model 204 assembled by Agusta. The first aircraft, designated AB204B — the suffix denoting a second version of the design after Bell's own — was completed by Agusta and flown for the first time on 10 May 1961.

The agreement with Agusta was only part of Bell's overseas co-operation programme then coming to fruition. Negotiations with the West German Government included a visit to Fort Worth by Chancellor Konrad Adenauer on 27 April. Flying appropriately enough in a UH-1, he was accompanied by President Lyndon Johnson. Talks were also being held with the Mitsui Co of Japan for the manufacture of the commercial Model 204 in that country.

Agusta established the 204 production line at its Cascina Costa plant, situated alongside Malpensa

International Airport, some 20 miles from Milan. Helicopter assembly was (and still is) spread over a variety of different sized buildings which did not appear to be ideal for the purpose. Agusta however quickly established a very high standard of workmanship for the aircraft it built, initially concentrating on the supply of AB204s to replace the large fleet of Italian Army Bell 47s. There was also a requirement by the Italian Navy that led to the first of two European UH-1 variants that had no direct equivalent in the output of the parent company's design department. These were the anti-submarine warfare models which were built in both single and twin-engined form.

As with the majority of Hueys purchased outside the USA, AB204s were used by the Italian Army mainly for liaison, rescue and general transport duties which gave increased versatility in the support of ground forces. A comprehensive range of armament sub-systems was developed to accommodate both American and European weapons, although the attack helicopter concept did not have initially a high priority in Italian Army planning.

Italian Navy requirements were however concerned with attack capability from the outset. Agusta had earlier developed the AB47J-3 for maritime deployment from frigates and subsequently built the A106 lightweight armed helicopter. As a replacement for the AB47, the 204 AS offered ample space for a range of detection equipment as well as a more lethal punch in the form of anti-shipping missiles and torpedoes.

Flying for the first time in 1965 the AB204 AS was powered by a single GE T58-GE-3 turboshaft of 1,290shp for take-off in multi-mission configuration (including armament) at a weight of 9,501lb. It offered a one hour 40 minute on-station time for search operations, estimated by a mission profile of 50% hovering out of ground effect and 50% cruise at an all-up weight (AUW) of 9,000lb. Operational radius was 60nm. For anti-submarine search and attack the aircraft carried sonar which could be stabilised during search operations, optional AN/APN-195 search radar and two Mk 44 homing torpedoes. For anti-fast patrol boat work a Bendix AN/AQS-13B search radar was linked to AS12 or similar missiles. Auxiliary fuel tanks could be fitted, as could a rescue hoist and emergency flotation gear.

The AB204 was in production until 1974, customers for the ASW version being the Italian and Spanish Navies. Standard versions found customers around the world, as can be seen from the listing at the end of this book, although newer versions have now generally superseded the 204.

Development of the Model 204 into the 205/UH-1D by Bell was paralleled by Agusta with the AB205 military version and AB205A-1 for the civilian market. The greater capacity of this version enabled Agusta to offer an even wider range of equipment to military customers. This included many items which were compatible with the earlier model such as a cargo suspension system, electro-mechanical hoist, fixed floats and snow skids.

Among the armament combinations were the M-21 Mamee system which comprised a 7.62mm Emerson minigun with its over-turret ammunition pod used in conjunction with an Emerson fixed seven-tube 2.75in rocket launcher, and Agusta's quad MG-3 twin rocket system, the result of collaboration with Rheinmetall of

Germany. The latter system consisted of two RM MG-3 machine guns and either a 2.75in seven-tube rocket launcher or Oerlikon 80mm launcher on each side turret mounting. A Spectrolab Nightsun searchlight in two types weighing either 25lb or 160lb was also available for cabin mounting and operation from the helicopter's standard electrical source.

Finding ready customers in the Middle East, Africa and Europe, the AB205 served the Italian armed forces and those countries which were already customers for the 204, a production rate of 12 machines per month being achieved by 1977. Agusta fitted the Lycoming T53-L-13 engine in later production models and with IFR — in-flight repair — and night flying instrumentation, the aircraft carried only one pilot for normal operations.

Below:
Excellent detail view of the Rolls-Royce Gnome powerplant of the AB204 being inspected on c/n 3154/4D-BL of No 1 Helicopter Wing, Austrian Air Force. *Mike Hooks*

The 'Isfahan' was developed because of Iran's need for a model tailored to the 'hot and high' conditions of the Middle East. As a follow-up to substantial Imperial Iranian Army orders for the Model 214A for trooping and heavy lift transport roles, the Air Force ordered 39 similar machines for the air-sea rescue role. This is the third machine delivered, 4-9422.   Bell

In 1968 Bell announced that the Canadian government had approved development of a twin-engined UH-1 to be powered by a Pratt & Whitney Aircraft of Canada PT6T-3 powerplant. The Twin Turbo Pac can be seen clearly on this Canadian Armed Forces' CUH-1N (now designated CH-135). *Bell*

Above:
An AB204B of the Italian Air Force in November 1966 during rescue operations in the flooded Belluno Province region. The fuselage markings indicate *31° Stormo*, the unit charged with VIP flying. Natural metal finish was short-lived on Italian Air Force Hueys. *Gregory Alegi*

Right:
Heavily laden Italian Army AB204 hauls a caravan 'on the hook' during relief operations.

Below:
A Swedish Army AB204 test-firing an AB Bofors RB53 Bantam wire-guided anti-tank missile. *Barry Wheeler*

Left:
Like Bell-built versions, Agusta Model 205s can carry a wide variety of weapons such as the 42-rocket launchers seen here. *Bruce Robertson*

Above:
An early AB205 on flight test with dual military markings and civil registration. *Agusta*

Below:
C/n 3039/4D-BA was also on the strength of Austria's No 1 Helicopter Wing prior to being replaced by AB212s after 1981. *Mike Hooks*

Above:
AH-1G 70-16004 of 'D' Troop, 8th Squadron, 3rd Cavalry Regiment, displaying its distinctive shark's teeth.
B. J. Zirkle via R. L. Ward

Below:
Armourers carry 2.72in rockets to a HueyCobra in Vietnam. *Bell*

Top:
**The revised lines of the AH-1T are shown well in this fine
view of BuAer No 160105 in current US Marine Corps
markings.** *Bell*

Above:
**While the Marines have the Tango model, the Army's latest
(and last) Cobra is the Sierra model. Salient features of these
updated Cobras are the flat-plate canopy, wide chord rotor
blades and the engine efflux exhaust suppressor. It seems
that current technology pays little heed to cleanness of line,
but the AH-1S still retains something of the sleekness of the
original HueyCobra, far more so than its successor, the
dramatically ugly AH-64 Apache.** *Bell*

Above:
Nice shot of a Peruvian Navy AB212 AS, one of six currently operated. *Mike Hooks*

Research into a twin engine installation for the AB205 led in the summer of 1967, to the 205BG, the suffix letters denoting the two Rolls-Royce Gnome H1200 shaft turbines coupled to a common reduction gear to give a maximum rating of 1,250shp each. The BG — Bi-Gnome — version was also able to take a pair of T58-GE-3s, and a further refinement was the AB205 TA with twin Aztazou XIIs, each of 700shp, or P&W (UAC) PT-6s or Continental 217s.

These interim models led to the Agusta version of the Bell Model 212 and a second ASW development for the Italian Navy, incorporating more sophisticated search equipment and heavier armament. Agusta carried out a major programme of modifications to the structure of the 205 to adapt it to the ASW role, mainly to permit the installation of sonar and radar. The sonar hoist was installed in a specially water-proofed corner of the cargo area with provision for easy maintenance access and removal of the hoist cable reel. Part of the cargo floor was removed to accommodate the well for the sonar transducer and the funnel, which housed the transducer and prevented water from entering the aircraft was designed for quick disassembly, enabling conversion to passenger or medvac configuration.

These modifications necessitated a completely new left hand door with a single window rather than two. The familiar hinged panel forward of the door was removed in favour of the single door incorporating a jettisonable emergency panel. The radar display was situated on the right hand side of the cabin, with the operator's seat facing rearwards. To enable the operator to abandon the machine in an emergency, the right hand doors incorporated a jettisonable panel adjacent to his seat, and a second emergency panel integral with the door.

To enable the radar antenna to be positioned on the roof, the fuselage was modified and strengthened to bear the weight of the rescue hoist and to allow for installation of an access panel used for removal and repositioning of the sonar hoist. Radical changes were also made to the main transmission cowling to allow room for the radar receiver and transmitter, ac generator and hydraulic reservoirs. Other necessary modifications were made to the flight controls, fuel system and electrics to enable the AB212 ASW/ASV to undertake a variety of tasks including submarine search, classification and strike; ASV search and strike; SAR; reconnaissance; troop transport and fire support; liaison; vertical replenishment; offensive and passive ECM early warning; and stand-off missile launch.

A comprehensive electronics fit offered the crew data link UHF, HF and VHF/AM and FM communications, Tacan, Doppler, UHF/VHF homer and radar altimeter navigation, plus search radar, AQS-18 dipping sonar and magnetic anomaly detector for

target acquisition and search. For ECM a range of
offensive jamming modes plus chaff was available,
with Programme Radar Warning, Electromagnetic
Pulse Direction Finder and analyser for passive ECM.

Armament of the AB212, which entered Italian
Navy service in 1976, includes a range of torpedoes
such as the Mks 44 and 46, Motofides 244AS and
TP42, depth charges, and up to four wire-guided,
optically-tracked Aerospatiale AS12 ASMs. The type
can also carry Martel Mk II anti-shipping 'fire and
forget' missiles or Sea Skua ASM and is equipped to
carry out hunter-killer missions against surface targets
using missiles and ECM.

Agusta followed the 212 with the AB412 Griffon
general purpose helicopter powered by the P&W
PT6T-3B providing 1,800shp as a collective unit.
Armament of the Griffon includes SNORA rockets
integral with markers that show target distance, TOW
— Tube-mounted, Optically sighted, Wire guided —
and guns up to and including 25mm cannon, the latter
weapon being developed in collaboration with
Oerlikon. For self-protection the AB412 is designed to
take an exhaust suppression kit developed by Piaggio.

The latest Cobra version at the time of writing is the AH-1T Plus SuperCobra, the first of which had a highly appropriate paint scheme. *Bell*

9.
Hueys for the World

Japan

A second UH-1 production line was established outside the USA in 1962 when the Mitsui Co undertook manufacture of the Model 204 in Japan. The firm was licensed by Bell on 20 January, and first deliveries were to civil operators. But the need to acquire modern tactical helicopters by the Japanese Ground Self Defence Force led to an arrangement whereby Fuji Heavy Industries built UH-1Bs under sub-licence from Mitsui at its plant at Utsonomiya. An order for 36 UH-1Bs was placed under the 2nd Defence Build-up Plan (DBP) of procurement for all Japan's armed forces in the period 1961-64.

Powered by KT53 engines (assembled by Kawasaki Aircraft from Lycoming supplied parts and identified as such by the prefix K), these early Fuji-Bell UH-1s equipped five independent squadrons directly attached to the GSDF's five Army Command headquarters. Production began in 1963 and all 36 machines had been delivered by December 1967, towards the end of the 2nd DBP. Further orders brought the total to 90, all of which had been delivered by 31 December 1970. The intention was to procure another 44 by 1973, 85 aircraft having been delivered by the spring of that year out of a requirement for 171. However, budget fluctuations and restrictions on the number of military aircraft allowed for in any one year were, and continue to be, a common occurrence in Japan. These factors meant that no more than 85 UH-1Bs actually entered service, inventory stabilising at about 83 for a number of years. The majority were based in the Japanese home islands, although two UH-1Bs were part of the initial force build-up on the island of Okinawa when this was returned to Japanese control on 15 May 1973.

Although Japanese UH-1Bs were not normally configured as gunships, Fuji evaluated six B models in the attack role in 1974. That spring a series of tests were undertaken with aircraft carrying two pods of 19×17mm rockets. The successful results of these trials led to an announcement that 20 UH-1s of each *Homen Herikoputa-Tai* would be equipped with rockets in the short term and later be equipped with TOW missiles.

Fuji's experimental department also test flew an interesting version of the UH-1B. This was the XMH, (in concept not unlike Bell's own YUH-1B compound), part of the programme to investigate future military helicopter performance and configurations. A company-owned aircraft, the XMH had small 22ft 3in-span wings to unload the main rotor, plus an extra horizontal stabilising surface. Design work started in July 1968 and construction was completed in January 1970. The XMH prototype (JA9009) flew for the first time on 11 February that year.

Phase I testing lasted until January 1973 after 87 flights had been made and the XMH had achieved a maximum speed of 185mph in a shallow dive, in April 1972. A further series of tests had been planned under Phase II evaluation which included the installation of turbojets — either two Teledyne CAE J69s of 1,540lb solid thrust each or a single Ishikawajime J3 of 2,645lb static thrust. It was estimated that jet power would push the rotorcraft to a maximum speed of over 200mph (219mph being quoted) compared to the Phase I maximum. In the event Phase II tests were never conducted, as all XMH flight testing was discontinued early in January 1973.

In late 1973 Fuji-built UH-1Hs began to supplement the UH-1Bs in Japanese service. The first example flew on 17 July 1973, the type being identical to American H models apart from a tractor-type tail rotor and 1,400shp KLT53-K-13B engines. The initial order was for 67 aircraft, the first three of which were handed over to the GSDF on 29 September 1973; 75 examples were in service by mid-1983 and follow-on orders are expected to keep the Fuji production lines open for at least the next five years. Annual procurement is deliberately limited and spread over a number of years: three aircraft were delivered in FY 80 and five in FY 81, and in the current fiscal year the budget has allowed for seven UH-1Hs against a requirement for eight.

The Japanese are now into their 1983-87 procurement programme, which allows for another 53 UH-1Hs, a total of 131 including the 78 purchased prior to 1982. Numbers in service at any given time understandably vary, but reports indicate that attrition rate in GSDF service has been acceptably low. Fuji's overhaul and repair centre has returned a number of damaged aircraft to service during the ground force's two decades of association with the UH-1.

In the mid-1970s, the GSDF looked ahead to its helicopter requirements for the late 1980s and 1990s, with particular emphasis on adding more punch to the

Above:
Japanese Ground Self-Defence Force Fuji UH-1Bs at Misawa Air Base, September 1975. *George Pennick*

relatively small numbers it actually receives. An attack type was of particular interest and the FY 77 and FY 78 budgets allowed the purchase of two Bell AH-1S HueyCobras for evaluation in the anti-armour role. It was found that this type more than met Japanese requirements and procurement financing was requested for deliveries in the early 1980s. But no provision for armed helicopters was made in the FY 81 budget, with the result that the lead time has been extended. The AH-1S was reinstated in the 1982 budget and the current procurement programme is for deliveries to operational units to start this year, although the requested number of aircraft has been reduced. Originally the 1982 budget allowed for 12 machines costing $106million for delivery in 1983; this figure was reduced to 10 and then five, with five planned for 1984 and six in 1985.

Some 30% of components will be locally produced for the first Fuji-assembled AH-1S, rising to about 70% from aircraft number nine. Current operational plans call for three squadrons to have TOW Cobras from 1985, the total requirement being 75 machines. To date, 14 of these have been purchased and follow-on orders could add as many as 50. Having standardised on TOW armament for their Cobras, 448 missiles are being procured by the Japanese.

West Germany
Almost exactly a year after Konrad Adenaur's tour of the Bell plant, negotiations bore fruit with a West German parliamentary committee's decision to buy the UH-1D as the new utility helicopter for the German armed forces, on 5 April 1965. Bonn ordered

Below:
Excellent view of a Luftwaffe UH-1D of HTG64 during a recent NATO exercise. *RAF Germany*

406 machines at a cost of approximately $125 million and, under the terms of the agreement with Bell, Dornier AG at Oberpfaffenhofen was to undertake licence manufacture of these helicopters as soon as was practicable. A three-phase programme was planned, originally calling for assembly and flight test of the first 10 machines (built by Bell under Phase I) after which they would be shipped to Dornier as components. Phase II called for Dornier to undertake final assembly of the next 40 aircraft (also manufactured by Bell as major sub-assemblies) and Phase III was the complete manufacture of UH-1Ds in Germany, apart from some dynamic components which would continue to be supplied by Bell.

In the event there was some modification to the programme, principally in the number of aircraft involved, and the potential customers. The total was reduced to 389, and included 26 for police border patrol work, 204 for the German Army and 27 for the Bundesmarine.

Economic considerations resulted in a further reduction, cutting the number of police machines and eliminating those for the Navy. Only two aircraft were supplied by Fort Worth, one new UH-1D and an ex-US Army example, s/n 61-701. These were given Dornier c/ns 7001 and 7002 respectively and four aircraft were assembled by Dornier with c/ns 7037-7040, a further two (7003 and 7036) being cancelled.

Between 1968 and 1971 Dornier built another 344 UH-1Ds, all aircraft except 16 for the police, going to the Luftwaffe and the Army. The Army received the original 204 aircraft, deliveries commencing on 1 August 1967, and the Air Force 140, including four for the *Flugbereitschaftstaffel (FBS)*. The last machine was delivered on 19 January 1971 and by July the UH-1 had equipped four *Staffeln* of HTG64 at Landsberg. At that time three *Staffeln* moved to Ahlhorn, HTG64 having previously undertaken a major SAR role which was continued after the base relocation, with two machines each stationed at Bremgarten, Hopsten, Jever, Neuberg, Norvenich and Pferdsfeld.

In the interim period, the German Hueys have given good service; Dornier has used examples to test various items of new equipment, including an airborne minelaying system which ejects mines from magazines mounted on outriggers, and the SIGINT airborne signal intelligence system. As part of this programme, a UH-1D was fitted out as a sensor platform to carry AEG-Comint (communications intelligence) aerials and receivers.

Extensively evaluated in the early 1980s, SIGINT helicopter flight trials were aimed at finding a suitable support platform for a next generation fixed-wing surveillance aircraft designed to provide early warning of an attack by Warsaw Pact forces along Germany's borders. A helicopter-borne system will give the army short-range signals capability for use at corps level to determine the number, location and strength of enemy communications. The system will also provide ELINT — electronic intelligence — on the number of opposing forces equipped with missiles; artillery strengths and details of radar-based reconnaissance.

The requirements of SIGINT include determining useful ranges, establishing reception and direction-finding facilities, signal processing and display and integration into Army command and control structure. Five companies have developed systems for the programme. Information published by Dornier depicts a UH-1D with a receiver operator seated on the left side of the cabin facing a bank of displays and instrumentation occupying the full width of the cabin, a large sensor fitted on the port side outrigger and extra aerials atop the transmission cowling and under the nose.

An important contract for Dornier in 1978 was the conversion of 62 European-based US Army AH-1Gs to AH-1S standard — leading to some speculation that the Germany Army might have ordered the Huey-Cobra to fulfil an attack helicopter requirement. But by late 1983 no decision had been reached — apart from the fact that the design chosen will be of European rather than American origin. But although Germany is not likely to operate the AH-1S, it has received sustantial quantities of TOW missiles. Some months before first deliveries, the UH-1 was involved in firing tests of the missile at the Munsterlager range in northern Germany.

An Unofficial Customer

As the earlier Hueys began to be replaced either by later Bell designs, or those of other manufacturers, in the world's leading air arms, countries with smaller military forces were ready customers for secondhand examples. And the recipients were not always in a position to buy direct through normal channels. A case in point was Rhodesia, which was subject to an international arms embargo after UDI but nevertheless received 11 ex-Israeli AB205s in 1978.

When put up for disposal by the Israelis the helicopters were sold to Air Associates of Chicago but were then purchased by the Singapore company Jamson Aviation while still in Israel. A US export licence was granted to Jamson to ship the 205s to PT Aero Survey of Indonesia, via Singapore. Their intended purpose at their destination was 'logging operations' — only PT Aero did not exist, unbeknown to the US Department of Commerce, which issued a licence within a few days of request without checking any details. The helicopters were duly shipped from Haifa to Durban, South Africa where they were unloaded and delivered to Rhodesia.

10.
Slimline Killer

In 1958, eight years or so before Vietnam war escalation revealed an urgent need for a purpose-built attack helicopter, Bell had explored this possible future requirement with the experimental D245 Combat Reconnaissance Helicopter. And although the 7292nd ACRP (Prov) trials also envisaged a probable role for such a machine, there was little official support at the time. Development of an attack helicopter was among the recommendations made by the Army Tactical Mobility Requirements Board's 1962 report, but only as one duty — of a multi-role helicopter. This idea persisted for a while and was at variance with that of a 'pure' attack helicopter.

Bell continued work, funding its own research and in June 1962 the company unveiled a mock-up of a machine that if built, would utilise a high percentage of UH-1 components. This was the D255, the Iroquois Warrior. Army officials invited to view it at Fort Bragg noted several new features including tandem seating for a two-man crew (the pilot being behind the gunner), mid-fuselage stub wings, and armament consisting of a turret faired into the extreme nose plus an underbelly weapons pod. The stepped tandem cockpit not only offered unparalleled visibility to both crew members but an extremely narrow fuselage cross section, similar to contemporary fighter cockpits. Indeed, the Warrior was called a 'fighter helicopter' by some observers who saw in it similar potential.

Sound as the concept appeared to be, the US Army had only recently begun to evaluate the armed utility helicopter — the fighter equivalent was a quantum leap that had to wait its time. Nevertheless, the Army did provide funding for R&D to continue, allocating $4 million from its FY 1964 budget to be spent on an 'armed attack helicopter'. It was the first time such an appropriation had been made for this purpose — and almost immediately it fuelled the USAF's case against organic Army aviation in the close support role. The Army had other problems as well. If it went ahead

with an attack helicopter, could it justify it? Other helicopters then being evaluated were either multi-role or specialised heavy lift types which it was argued (with considerable justification) had far more use potential than machines designed purely to fight. Apart from a secondary training mission, it was feared that an attack helicopter would be redundant in a non-hostile environment. This fact did not escape the Secretary of the Army, who temporarily shelved the project early in 1963. Not that the Secretary was against an attack helicopter in principle — on the contrary he felt that an improved design, faster than the 155mph top speed quoted by the original specification, was what was wanted. Bell stuck to its 'single purpose' design philosophy while other companies attempted to woo the Army with existing designs adapted to the attack role. Among them was Kaman with its UH-2 Tomahawk, evaluated by the Army in 1963-64.

In the meantime Bell constructed a flying test bed of the Iroquois Warrior, having been given the go-ahead in December 1962. To keep costs down the company reconfigured an OH-13 airframe for the purpose. Designated the Model 207 Sioux Scout the aircraft was built around a Lycoming TVO-435-B1A supercharged piston engine, as fitted to the OH-13S. The forward fuselage and tailboom were faired in and the transmission and tail rotor were borrowed from a commercial Model 47J-2. Although appearing rotund, the forward fuselage was only 39in wide (compared with 38in at widest point in the AH-1G) and employed similar boxbeam honeycomb panel covered construction that would be used in the HueyCobra. The two man crew sat in tandem, the seats being stepped to provide maximum field of vision for both occupants. Dual controls were fitted, those for the front seat gunner comprising armchair type hand controls for cyclic, pitch, collective pitch and elevator movement. The 'half shell' canopy terminated in a clear nose cone extending the full depth of the fuselage, protruding over the barrels of two M-60 machine guns set in a hefty Emerson Electric ventral turret.

Flying for the first time in July 1963 with registration N73927, the Sioux Scout was extensively flown for the next 16 months. It undertook a nationwide demonstration tour of Army bases before passing to the 11th Air Assault Division for evaluation in January 1964. The reports were enthusiastic: the stub wings set behind the canopy helped give the Scout a manoeuvrability, rate of climb and speed far superior to any previous Model 47/H-13 and the greater accuracy of the line-of-sight guns confirmed turret armament for attack helicopters. Designed primarily to hold fuel cells, the small wings were also fitted with stores hardpoints during the test period. The 11th AAD recommended development of a helicopter based on the Scout, but preferred a turbine engine.

That same year the Army attempted to go a step or two beyond the 'basic' attack helicopter by formulating its Advanced Aerial Fire Support System (AAFSS). Circulated to industry in the latter part of 1964, the AAFSS was a demanding requirement for a long range helicopter gunship with high performance. From the submissions of a dozen manufacturers, the Army chose two, the Lockheed AH-56 Cheyenne and the Sikorsky S-66 Blackhawk, for development to prototype stage. While furthering the helicopter state of the art, neither design reached production status and it eventually fell to Bell to 'fill the gap' — a gap which lasted nearly 20 years — with the 'interim' HueyCobra. It was late 1983 before the next generation helicopter gunship entered production in the shape of the Hughes AH-64 Apache.

In 1964 Bell looked again at the Iroquois Warrior; it was decided that the proposed airframe was too large for the Lycoming T53 and a scaling-down exercise was initiated to meet either the Aerial Scout requirement then being formulated by the Army, or the

Below:
The distinctive lines of the Sioux Scout, forerunner of the HueyCobra. *Bell*

AAFSS. The Warrior redesign became the D262 and despite it being eliminated from the AAFSS competition Bell decided in January 1965 to build a prototype. As the Model 209, design and construction began in March under the direction of Project Engineer J. R. Duppstadt.

Many design features of the Model 209 had already been well proven on the UH-1 or Sioux Scout, including the 540 rotor system, the cambered vertical fin, tandem seating and so forth. As Bell pointed out to the Army, use of existing components offered numerous advantages, not least of which were low lead time and economy in production. Tooling-up time would be minimal and pilot and maintenance staff training could be completed quickly. Most important of all, the Model 209 could be deployed to Vietnam without delay.

During design, Bell considered additional propulsion from auxiliary engines, but decided that a pure helicopter would be a far simpler solution to a now urgent Army need than anything more radical. The company also considered another 'future feature' for armed helicopters, a retractable landing gear. The necessary mechanism was developed and incorporated into the first aircraft but the marginal performance

advantage did not warrant the increased risk of damage in an emergency landing and higher maintenance time, and only the first machine had retractable skids.

When the Vietnam war intensified in 1965, the Army had to choose between continuing the AAFSS programme and selecting a suitable type for production late in the year *if* one could be found, or simplifying the requirement. Alternatively, an 'interim AAFSS' could be sought. The decision was a compromise — to continue the original AAFSS while seeking a simpler option. In August 1965 a US Army Material Command meeting chaired by Col Harry L. Bush studied five companies' proposals in a competition that required an operational airframe to be ready in 24 months. The board examined the Kaman UH-2, Sikorsky S-61, Boeing-Vertol CH-47A, Piasecki Model 16H and the Bell Model 209.

Only Bell proposed a completely new airframe, all others being adaptions of existing designs. Piasecki's was the most revolutionary, the 16H Pathfinder having a propeller vane arrangement in a 'ring tail' fairing, stub wings and a single rotor. A development proposed adding two T58 engines to create a true compound helicopter. The largest type studied was Boeing's mighty Chinook, four armed examples of which had already been ordered for evaluation.

Having initiated construction, any disadvantage Bell's Model 209 could have faced in meeting the deadline was eliminated and a presentation was made to the Bush Board on 18 August. The prototype (N209J) was rolled out on 3 September 1965 and shop completed the following day. The first ground runs took place on 7 September, with the first flight that same day.

The prototype Model 209 featured a ventral extension to the vertical fin and was powered by the T53-L-11 of 1,100shp. The higher-rated L-13 was installed in the second aircraft and the ventral fin dispensed with during testing. Fitted to enhance directional stability during autorotation, it was found to be unnecessary. On 25 October the Model 209 flew at a sustained speed cruise of 200mph and thereby substantially exceeded the official world speed record for a helicopter in its weight class, which them stood at 180.1mph (289.781km/hr). The Army was extremely impressed with the new attack helicopter's performance and it appeared that Bell might receive a construction contract without any comparative flight tests with the Sikorsky and Kaman proposals, Piasecki having been eliminated. But a comparison test was called for and was held at Edwards AFB between 13 November and 1 December 1965.

Declared the winner of the Edwards tests, the Model 209 was the subject of an Army contract for two preproduction prototypes, signed on 4 April 1966. On

Below:
The long-lived AH-1G prototype flight tested most of the HueyCobra's weapons and systems, including Hughes TOW missiles. It is seen here with early podded launch tubes and a laser rangefinder in the nose. *Bell*

13 April Bell received an Army order for 110 aircraft, designated UH-1H. This designation was subsequently allocated to the refined UH-1D and the Model 209 became the AH-1G HueyCobra, the 'attack' prefix more accurately reflecting its mission. The suffix letter was the next in sequence after UH-1F, although the name was a departure from Army practice of using Indian names for aircraft. The word 'Cobra', already used to identify armed UH-1s, became more of a generic term for Bell gunships and was perpetuated in other models. One had only to see an AH-1G to know that the name was eminently suitable.

Company flight testing continued to show the excellent handling and performance capabilities of the AH-1, including a maximum dive speed of 219mph, an initial climb rate of 1,580ft/min and a service ceiling of 12,700ft. Armament initially consisted of an Emerson TAT-102 nose turret with a single GE XM-134 7.62mm rotating six barrel gun with a firing rate of 4,000 rounds/min. The turret offered azimuth coverage of 230°, elevation of 25° and deflection of 65° and could also be adapted to accommodate a 40mm grenade launcher. The 9ft 4in span stub wings were stressed to take a variety of ordnance on up to four hardpoints. Crew protection was provided by Philco-Aeronutronic Ausform armour plating made of two thin, light steel alloy sheets welded together; the outer sheet of plating was designed to break bullets into fragments while the inner sheet prevented fragments from penetrating. Both crew seats were also made of Ausform and there were armour-plated side panels

which could be raised or lowered to about shoulder height on both sides of each man and locked in place.

In the spring of 1967 N209J was taken on an extensive tour of Europe in conjunction with Agusta, Bell's European representative. The aircraft was demonstrated to military authorities in most of Europe's capitals after making its debut at the 1967 Paris Salon. Much of the demonstration flying was in the capable hands of Clem Bailey, Bell's chief production test pilot, who invited aviation writers to gain a first-hand impression of the machine. During its tour, which ended in the UK in July, the Model 209 flew well over 600 hours, nearly 150 of which were during and after the Paris show, with little opportunity for extensive maintenance. It performed admirably throughout the tour which took in visits to British Army helicopter units at Middle Wallop, Odiham and Old Sarum, the Royal Naval Air Station Lee-on-Solent and A&AEE Boscombe Down.

Among the impressions of the HueyCobra published at that time was the fact that the new Bell design was 'as different from the UH-1 as chalk is from cheese. Many helicopters, even of different makes and different configurations, are quite similar to fly but the HueyCobra is in a new class of its own.'

Below:
After its debut at the 1967 Paris Air Show, N209J went on a European demonstration tour. Whilst in Britain, it visited the HQ of the Army Air Corps at Middle Wallop.
Museum of Army Flying

Above:
A British photographer took 'round-the-clock' views of the Cobra at Middle Wallop, including this dramatic head-on shot to illustrate the Bell gunship's small frontal area.
Museum of Army Flying

Right:
The same photographer took this view of the gunner's sighting station in N209J. *Museum of Army Flying*

11.
Vietnam Cobras

In order to absorb the HueyCobra into Army air operations as quickly as possible, Material Command established NETT — New Equipment Training Team — for the AH-1G at St Louis, Missouri, on 1 August 1966. Project Officer and Team Leader was Maj Paul F. Anderson. Almost exactly a year later, on 29 August 1967, the first AH-1Gs were on their way to Vietnam. Six aircraft, plus one UH-1D, left Fort Worth bound for Bien Hoa, accompanied by 50 hand-picked combat experienced US Army pilots, mechanics and other specialists. Behind these men lay almost 12 months of intensive work at the Bell plant while HueyCobras were coming off the line. They were able to observe production methods, and even suggest a few changes; they participated fully in the Army qualification trials for the new helicopter gunship and successfully completed the first phase of the task. Phase II was in-theatre training for personnel of the first Vietnam-based combat units that would introduce the new type to action. The NETT was due to spend 12 months in SE Asia.

At 17.07hrs on 31 August 1967, the AH-1G made its first Vietnam flight, with Lt-Col Anderson and Maj Nick Stein at the controls. Four days later, on 4 September, Maj-Gen P. Seneff Jr, accompanied by Chief Warrant Officer W2 J. D. Thomson, flew the first combat sortie in 66-15263. Seneff was then commander of the 1st Aviation Brigade and keen to see what the new arrival could do, although the flight was only logged as a routine orientation sortie. But when the Cobra chanced on a fire-fight in progress 10 miles northeast of Can Tho City in the Mekong Delta, it was too inviting a chance to pass up. The slim gunship joined UH-1s engaging an enemy force hiding on a small island; after several passes by the helicopters, the Viet Cong decided to withdraw and took to a number of small boats, easy meat for the prowling rotorcraft. Seneff selected one and attacked with the minigun and rockets. Afterwards, the crew was officially credited

with the HueyCobra's first kill of the war — one sampan destroyed and four Viet Cong killed, although neither crewman was sure that's what they had achieved. Nevertheless, the AH-1G had been blooded.

As more Cobras arrived in Vietnam they were issued to the first operational unit, the 1st Platoon, 334th Armed Helicopter Company (AHC) — the famed 'Playboys' and the most experienced formation of its kind in Vietnam, having been instrumental in introducing the UH-1 to combat some five years before. On 8 October two 334th Cobras, piloted by Capt Kenneth Rubin and WO Robert Bey with gunners WO John Ulsh and Richard Wydur, flew an escort mission to UH-1 'slicks' of the 118th AHC. So good was the Cobras' fire support at the LZ that the 10 Hueys landed without any enemy opposition. Later that day, the same aircraft destroyed four heavily-bunkered enemy fortifications and sank 14 sampans, these vessels being torn to pieces by the fire from the turret guns.

The performance of the AH-1G in Vietnam was closely monitored by Bell, using crew reports furnished by NETT and recorded data obtained during combat sorties. Flight recorders to measure a list of operating factors including airspeed, centre of gravity vertical acceleration, main rotor rpm, air temperature and the behaviour of armament systems, were fitted. Designed for simplicity, reliability and with minimum maintenance, the recorders were of the photopanel type which incorporated a camera mounted in the centre of a duplicated flight instrument display. The camera photographed itself through a mirror every 30 seconds in normal flight, and every second during firing runs, and continued for five seconds after firing had ceased.

Below:
At least two of the AH-1Gs taken to Vietnam by the Cobra New Equipment Training Team (NETT) were camouflaged in USAF tan, dark green and white, one being 66-15259 seen at Vung Tau. It also bears a white kangaroo 'zap', the handiwork of personnel of No 9 Squadron RAAF, which was based there. *via R. L. Ward*

Left:
AH-1G production in full swing in the late 1960s. *Bell*

Above:
AH-1G 67-152292 was part of the first major production
batch of 112 machines. The early Cobras were rushed to
Vietnam, where they proved superior to UH-1 gunships in
the fire support role. This aircraft has the early centreline
gun mounting in the turret and the emblem of the Transition
School on the rotorhead 'doghouse'. *Bell*

Below left:
Students at the US Army Cobra Transition School at Vung
Tau check out the AH-1G's cockpit during a pre-flight
inspection, 29 September 1970. *US Army*

Below:
A six-barrel minigun on a Sagami mount installed on a
UH-1B, Phu Loi, August 1969. Tests on AH-1Gs and the
UH-1B model showed that the minigun was the most used
weapon on Hueys. *USAF*

Early tests with the recorders, conducted on two AH-1Gs, one stationed at Bien Hoa and one at Can Tho, revealed some useful facts. Both the Cobras were engaged primarily on 'firefly' (sampan attack) missions. It was found, in 480 hours of monitoring, that the HueyCobras spent a considerable time above the power-on rpm limit of the T53-L-13 engine, and that the maximum load factor was 2.3g, incurred mostly during pullouts after gunnery runs. The data from these tests, which was ultimately extracted from the process film, computerised and stored on magnetic tape by Bell, also showed that the minigun was by far the most used weapon on the Cobra — and also on the UH-1C, which was subject to similar filmed flight recordings for comparison purposes. The test referred to above was an early example, but it was nevertheless recommended that it should continue to give the Army the equivalent of the Air Force Structural Integrity Programme for its helicopters. The results of such data assisted both the military and the manufacturers to 'improve the product'.

Below:
Patricia Ann, **an AH-1G from the 1st Cavalry Regiment, looking for trouble in a Vietnamese village. The Regiment's yellow crossed sabre emblem is just visible under the nose.** *Bell*

Right:
The ultra-slim lines of the AH-1G seen to advantage. In Vietnam the Viet Cong initially had trouble combatting the HueyCobra and troops were ordered not to fire at all. *Bell*

Although the AH-1Gs generally flew at 1,500ft, gunnery accuracy was found to be good even from 4,000ft altitude and the slim profile and higher speed of the aircraft meant that the enemy had extreme difficulty in tracking it. Quite often, he did not try. Such was the firepower of the Cobra that it was said that troops used to engaging the slower UH-1s which invariably avoided directly overflying defending guns were told 'Don't fire at the skinny helicopters'. With their diminutive profile and manoeuvrability, the Cobras could make fighter-like passes on enemy positions and overfly, relying on their speed to get them out of trouble.

While crews generally appreciated their potent new mounts, there were those who had reservations, especially men who had grown used to the extra eyes and firepower of two door gunners on the UH-1. It was found for example, that the enclosed cockpit hampered early warning of groundfire in close proximity. The cockpit was virtually sound-proof and it was extremely hard to detect the sound of gunfire — unless it was uncomfortably close. And the cockpit was also unbearably hot until a powerful air conditioner was fitted.

Issued to four principal types of unit in Vietnam — Air Cavalry Troops; Assault Helicopter Companies, Aerial Weapons Companies and Aerial Rocket Batteries — the AH-1G's basic missions in Vietnam were those of escort to UH-1 troop carriers, fire support to airmobile units, hunter-killer operations often in company with OH-6A Loach scout helicopters , and as a component of a 'Pink' fire team.

Distribution of the HueyCobra among units previously flying UH-1B/C gunships was accomplished fairly rapidly, although some units did not exchange their Hueys for Cobras before the US withdrawal from Vietnam; others received only one or two examples before pulling out — an event that was given some impetus by the 1968 Tet offensive. Tet proved to be the first major test for the HueyCobra under fire, the gunships playing a decisive role in the defence of Saigon, Long Binh and Bien Hoa. Maj-Gen Robert Williams, who replaced Maj-Gen Seneff as CO of the 1st Aviation Brigade, was fulsome in his praise for the Cobra's performance during those grim weeks. Even the Air Force was moved to comment that the AH-1G could 'do everything that a fighter plane can do'.

To the troops on the ground, it could do it better, simply because the armed helicopters could get in closer and deliver fire more accurately. The Bien Hoa base commander said of them: 'They swept down about two feet over our heads and fired into the enemy positions, knocking out the troops who had us pinned down. The Cobras were the turning point in the enemy's destruction'.

The Cobra's fire support was likened to that of a tank. When details of the Tet fighting were analysed, Gen Frank S. Besson Jr, commander of Material

Below:
Massed Cobras and a few Hueys tethered and parked at Norfolk Naval Base, Virginia prior to shipment to Europe for the annual Exercise 'Reforger' in the autumn of 1976.
US Army

Command stated: 'The Cobras were able to deliver fire, not just into buildings hiding VC, but into the specific windows of the rooms being used by the VC'.

The Army 'flying tanks' actually met tanks during the NVA's 1972 spring offensive. When An Loc was besieged, AH-1Gs of F Battery, 79th Aerial Field Artillery of the 1st Cavalry's 3rd Brigade destroyed or immobilised over 20 tanks and damaged a large variety of other vehicles, mostly with the trusty 2.75in rocket. But the opposition was by then fierce. It was an out-of-character gamble by the enemy to commit armour in the face of heavy US defences, but North Vietnamese firepower was considerable, consisting of SA-7 SAMS as well as radar-predicted AA artillery. The SA-7 is known to have claimed two Cobras during the fighting, which led the Army to hurriedly modify the AH-1G's exhaust system to reduce the infra-red signature. This took the form of an exhaust shield which directed the hot gases upwards to be dispersed by the rotor wash instead of streaming aft. There was some penalty in the anti-SAM device in that it marginally affected performace, with a knock-on stricture on the amount of wing stores that could be carried. Also, the missile threat force crews to fly lower than they had hitherto, somewhat nullifying the shallow dive attack which had become the most effective flight profile against most types of target.

As a result of Vietnam combat, the AH-1G had some modifications made to it during the course of production. The most important was switching the tail rotor from its original left hand side tail mounting to the right. Most Hueys had been found to be sensitive to quartering tail winds, particularly when backing out of revetment. They 'ran out of left pedal' and the HueyCobra with its taller tailfin, was worse than the UH-1 in this respect. Bell began changing the rotors to the right side during major rebuilds at the factory and in Vietnam, the modification involving a complete new tailboom in most, if not all cases. And of course, at first personnel would avoid getting too near to these machines when they were running because their tail rotor was on the 'wrong' side. . . . The change to right-hand side tail rotor was also made on the UH-1N during production and to USAF HH-1Hs and most civilian Hueys.

Changes were also made to the turret armament, the TAT-102 being substituted for the XM-28 turret mounting either twin miniguns (the TAT had only one centreline gun) or a grenade launcher. Above the turret, the twin landing lights in the extreme tip of the nose were removed in favour of a single retractable light underneath the nose.

To offset the SA-7 threat, the Army invested some $25million in infra-red RCM kit for its helicopter fleet, purchasing over 1,000 units for the machines operating in Vietnam, between 1967 and 1971. Both UH-1 and AH-1s were equipped with the ALQ-44 set, mounted on the engine cowling immediately in front of the exhaust. The equipment was very effective in defeating the SA-7 guidance system encountered in 1972.

The Army's HueyCobra programme was watched with great interest by the Marine Corps which was quickly convinced that it should procure its own. Consequently a request was made for 72, enough to equip one squadron in each of the three active air wings. The Secretary of the Navy approved the procurement in July 1967, although the Secretary of Defence downgraded this figure to a total of 38.

In February 1969 the first Marine AH-1Gs were delivered, five aircraft being handed over at Fort Worth. But since no flight training programme had been established, they were immediately loaned to the Army at Hunter Field, Georgia, so that Marine pilots could be trained on them. In three months the first Marine Cobra pilots had graduated and by the end of June 17 AH-1Gs were on Marine strength. Two were retained for R&D purposes and 10 were immediately despatched to Vietnam, where the first four arrived on 10 April for assignment to VMO-2.

Following a week of orientation flights, the first Marine Cobras sortie took place on 18 April. This medevac escort flight was followed by attack support missions, leading to a very favourable report on the first month's activity. Flying from Marble Mountain, the 1st MAW Cobras were the subject of combat evaluation from 10 May to 11 August 1969. By December VMO-2 had its full complement of 24 aircraft and on the 16th unit reorganisation of Marine helicopter units brought a new designation, HML-367.

Marine AH-1Gs stayed in Vietnam until on 26 May 1971, all units began to stand down prior to withdrawal. The single-engined Cobras did however, participate in Operation 'Lam Son 719', the incursion into Laos during February-April 1971, when they were usually paired with the new AH-1J SeaCobras, then beginning their operational evaluation.

12.
Refanged
Cobras

Important milestone though the HueyCobra was in Marine service, the Corps was conscious that its attack helicopters had, like its UH-1s, been primarily designed for Army use. The 'first generation' Marine Cobras had no rotor brake, a turret armament which was thought to be too light — and most important of all, no second engine. Although generally impressed with the AH-1G's performance, the Corps found its suitability for shipboard operation lacking.

Figures on USMC UH-1 operations during 1956-57 were revealing: the loss of 17 machines to combat damage or operational mishap was directly attributable to engine failure or malfunction. These statistics reinforced the view that a second engine was

paramount if the Cobra was to continue in amphibious operations. While it was nevertheless remembered that single-engined helicopters can carry out an auto-rotate, power-off controlled descent in the event of power failure, the resulting landing can still cause destruction of the aircraft if the chosen terrain is unsuitable for an emergency landing. The sea certainly came into that category.

It was though, one thing to be sure of the requirement and quite another to fulfil it; by early 1968 Corps commitments, particularly in Vietnam, necessitated staying with the single-engined AH-1G at least until the end of the war. Twin Cobras would be additional aircraft in USMC inventory and the old dictum that for every additional helicopter ordered, a fixed-wing machine had to be deleted from the budget, was still widely held. Consequently the FY 69 Defence Budget proposed the procurement of 38 'interim' AH-1J models. These machines had a rotor brake, Navy avionics and a 20mm gun in the chin turret — but they were still single-engined. Then came the 1968 Tet offensive in Vietnam. Indirectly, the enemy's startling show of strength was to give the Marines their twin-engined Cobra much sooner than expected.

Below:
The first of 38 Cobras for the Marines had BuAer numbers assigned but not used, the aircraft retaining their US Army serials. This one is 68-15038, third machine of the order.
Bell

Marine helicopter losses in the Tet fighting included a number of UH-1Es; those aircraft had to be replaced and the Corps was quick to point out that as it was also tasked to provide additional helicopters for the war effort, they might just as well be twin-engined Cobras. Bell had meanwhile produced the 'Twin Pack' UH-1 for Canada and had flown the civil Twin Two Twelve in the spring of 1969. A powerplant was therefore not only available for a new Marine Cobra, it could be fitted without exorbitantly high cost. Reassured by this fact, the Secretary of Defence persuaded Congress not only to divert funds from less urgent Marines Corps aircraft procurement into a twin Cobra (to be known as the SeaCobra) but also raise the number of aircraft to 49. It seemed however, that the Marine Corps' appropriation of armed helicopters was never to be without difficulty, for immediately this news was announced there arose a controversy over using Canadian engines in the SeaCobra. To appease those who believed that the aircraft should have American engines, a requirement was circulated among all eligible manufacturers, including United Aircraft of Canada, in April 1969. A month was given for reply. By May only United and Continental Aviation & Engineering Corp, an American manufacturer, had responded. Continental's proposed engine was suitable, but only United had powerplants in production and fully proven in flight test. The Canadian concern got the contract.

On 10 October 1969, Bell unveiled the first AH-1J at the Fort Worth plant in the presence of a group of Marine Officers which included Brig-Gen Victor A. Armstrong, past commander of HMR-161 in Korea and MAG-36 in Vietnam, and Col Edwin H. Finlayson, Head of Weapons Group, HQMC. These officers were delighted by the new machine, which was almost exactly the attack helicopter the Corps had originally wanted. It had the armament in the shape of an XM-197 turret with a three-barrelled 20mm gun firing at up to 750 rounds/min, plus stub wing stations stressed to take the XM-18 7.62mm minigun pod, the seven-tube XM-157 or the 19-tube XM-159 aerial rocket pod. The aircraft was also fitted with a rotor brake for shipboard operations, standard Navy avionics, and most important of all, twin engines.

There followed an extensive period of testing before the SeaCobra was cleared for operational service with the Corps, necessary because the aircraft was considerably different to the fully 'tried and tested' Army Cobras previously used without secondary evaluation by the Corps. The first four AH-1Js went to Paxutent River for Board of Survey and Inspection (BIS) trials in July 1970. Seven more arrived in September for crew and maintenance training with VMO-1. Some of these aircraft lacked parts of the armament system and were subsequently returned to Bell for completion.

Below:
Part of the Marines' first order for AH-1J SeaCobras, BuAer No 157788 poses with a UH-1. Camouflage painted, both aircraft were used as demonstrators by Bell. *Bell*

An urgent task was to test the SeaCobra under actual combat conditions, and on 12 February 1971, Col Paul W. Niesen, eight other officers and 23 enlisted Marines departed the US for Marble Mountain. Concurrently four AH-1Js were flown out in Air Force C-133s. The crews arrived in Vietnam on 16 February, the Cobras two days later. SeaCobra evaluation in Vietnam was under the jurisdiction of HML-367. On 22 February the first combat mission was flown when Col Niesen and Lt-Col Clifford E. Reese, HML-367's CO, accompanied AH-1Gs on support to transport helicopters around a hostile landing zone.

The four SeaCobras were kept busy in the next two months and by 28 April, when the evaluation was completed, they had flown a total of 614 hours. During the period, the quartet had also fired 14,950 rounds of 7.62mm ammunition, no less than 72,945 rounds of 20mm, and released 2,842 rockets. Other munitions had also been expended and the USMC Commandant's summary of the evaluation concluded that the AH-1J 'provides a significantly greater effectiveness in firepower over the AH-1G'.

Combat operations revealed two types of armament load for the AH-1J, 'light' or 'heavy' depending on the target likely to be encountered and the range require-

ments. A light load was 1,475lb of armament and consisted of the maximum amount of 20mm ammunition, 14×2.75in rockets and either gun pods or other light ordnance on the wing hardpoints. A heavy loading was 2,400lb — 300 rounds of 20mm and a total of 76 rockets. It was also found that the SeaCobra had a speed range of up to 155kt in level flight and up to 190kt in a dive. At maximum weight it could maintain altitude of 2,000ft even with one engine malfunctioning.

The same day that the SeaCobra evaluation team began operations in Vietnam, the first helicopter attack squadron, HMS-269, began to form at New River. The unit was the first of three such squadrons in the active Marine force and one in the reserves, the former becoming part of MAG-26. Flying UH-1Es until 7 April, when Bell delivered five AH-1Js, HMA-269 had another 23 Cobras by June 1970 and the unit was officially commissioned on 1 July.

With its unit complement of attack helicopters established for the time being, the Marine order for the AH-1J was raised to 124 aircraft. In the event, this procurement was not to be completed — at least with helicopters configured 'as ordered' because the advent of the Hughes TOW missile brought about a modified version after 67 AH-1Js had been delivered. This new version was the AH-1T, the development of which was to extend Cobra delivery time to the Marines by some seven years, for the conversion to TOW capability involved a number of major changes to the airframe, not least of which was a lengthened fuselage.

Below:

A major modification programme produced the Marines' AH-1T. This is the prototype during flight tests showing the longer fuselage and ventral fin. *Bell*

Bell received the go-ahead to modify the last two AH-1Js in the spring of 1974, a busy period, because it was also building Cobras for the US Army and fulfilling an order for AH-1Js placed by Iran. In addition, its R&D programme was concerned with the YAH-63 Advanced Attack Helicopter for the Army; there was an extensive civil programme underway and apart from JetRanger development, the company was also producing current versions of the UH-1. That year also saw Bell expansion 'on the ground' in the form of new production facilities. In January the company commissioned a $2million paint shop at the Hurst plant and in February 1974 a new $1.7million engineering test and evaluation centre was opened. A Bell Helicopter supply centre was established at Schipol East Airport in the Netherlands in March and on 23 April 1974, a ceremony at the Hurst plant marked the delivery of the 20,000th helicopter.

The specification for the improved AH-1J included substitution of a 1,970shp P&W T402 coupled engine in place of the standard 1,800shp T400 TwinPac, and a transmission rating of 2,050shp instead of 1,290shp formerly. Main rotor diameter was to be increased from 44ft to 48ft, with a blade chord increase from 27in to 33in, and there were to be improvements to the tail rotor.

As work proceeded, it became obvious that the additional weight of equipment necessary for the Cobra to carry out its anti-armour mission would adversely affect the aircraft's centre of gravity if no structural modifications were made. Infra-red suppressors, detectors, jammers and decoys all contributed to tail-heaviness and the consequent need to lengthen the aircraft. Under the Improved SeaCobra programme, Bell therefore proposed two solutions tailored to the Marines' budget considerations. The company built

two AH-1Js for testing in 1976, one a fully TOW-configured machine, the other a TOW-convertible aircraft. The Marines then planned to purchase 32 more TOW-convertible aircraft and then 24 TOW-configured examples with budgeting extending into 1977. Respective cost of each Cobra was $1.7million and $2.3million as a flyaway unit. By the spring of 1976, the order had been slightly revised to 33 TOW convertibles and purchasing extended to FY 78 for the final eight machine of the total order for 57. The first AH-1T flew in June 1976.

Externally, the new model could be distinguished from the AH-1J principally by its tailboom profile. Extended by 31in, this had a distinctive double kink along the underside, whereas the AH-1J's was a continuous line, and to aid directional stability a ventral fin was added. A 12in bay was also added aft of the cockpit bulkhead, this to allow for possible future growth without affecting the centre of gravity limitations.

Under the skin, the AH-1T incorporated the dynamic components of the Model 214 developed for Iran, the uprated engine also originally developed for the Iranian version of the AH-1J, and a number of detail improvements required by the Marine Corps. Model 214 dynamics included the 48ft diameter main rotor and the 8ft 8in tail rotor, the latter being positioned at the top of the fin in a manner similar to the UH-1C/D series rather than the fin mounting of all other Cobra models. Installed powerplant was the

P&W T400-WV-402 TwinPack coupled turboshaft rated at 1,970shp for take-off, enabling the new aircraft to not only offer a better performance at all altitudes and temperatures, but a 40% increase in maximum weight — to 14,000lb, as against 10,000lb for the AH-1J. The weight of fuel and disposable ordnance was almost three times as great as the AH-1J, at 5,392lb (2,523lb). The M-197 20mm gun turret was fitted as standard and a similar mix of stores as defined for the J model could be carried on stub wing hardpoints — with the significant addition of the Hughes TOW system, four tubes being carried on each side. Formal acceptance of the first of 48 AH-1T production aircraft was made during the Corps' annual Aviation Association Convention in Dallas on 15 October 1977 by Lt-Gen Thomas Miller, Deputy Chief of Staff for Aviation HQMC.

A further increase in AH-1T performance and capability started in 1980 when Bell produced the AH-1T Plus. Under a co-operative USMC programme, the company modified a bailed (leased) AH-1T to take the GE T-700 engine pack, with an installed rated power of 3,250shp and transmission rating of 1,050shp. Gross weight was raised to 15,000lb.

Bell first intalled the T700 in Novemebr 1979 using a Marine T model. As the pattern aircraft was a service helicopter, Bell first sought permission to make the installation and covered the cost of the conversion through its independent R&D funds. This prototype first flew in April 1980, achieving a level flight speed of 193mph. It was evaluated by Navy and Marine test pilots over a period of eight weeks after which it was returned to its original configuration.

The AH-1T Plus was flight tested by the Marines with the Rockwell Hellfire laser-guided anti-armour missile, which is expected to enter service in 1984. The missile has been flight test extensively on the AH-1T (standard version) and it is also to be retro-fitted to Marine AH-1Js. With about twice the range of current surface-to-surface anti-tank missiles such as TOW, Hellfire can be launched into two trajectories — low for use below cloudbase, or high, which requires remote designation. In the latter mode the missile is fired from the helicopter in defilade to climb over intervening terrain and dive on to its target. Marine SeaCobras will have only remote designation capability, a $50,000 package weighing 50lb and comprising a digital cockpit display, target heading indicator and a remote electronics box. High versatility is claimed by the manufacturers for Hellfire, which has been designed to accept infra-red imaging and millimetre wave seekers in conjunction with advanced target acquisition systems when these become available. Eight Hellfires are to be carried by the AH-1T.

By late 1981, deliveries of the AH-1T to the Marines had reached 51 machines, 23 of which had TOW capability, and Bell was then contracted to retrofit 28 more aircraft, the work being carried out at the Amarillo facility. First deliveries of these machines was made early in 1983. Currently, the Corps has 51 TOW AH-1Ts in inventory and it seems likely that additional modifications, if not more aircraft, will be required to fit Marine Cobras for an air defence role

Below:

The AH-1T Plus SuperCobra. This drawing shows the revised cowling contours of the T700 engine pack, the GTKA/A 20mm turret (the gun now qualified to use Phalanx rounds), the TOW electronics pack on the lower forward fuselage, and the wingtip stores stations for Sidewinder AAMs.

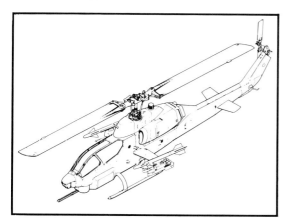

against other armed helicopters. Current USMC plans call for procurement of 44 AH-1Ts in FYs 84 and 85 to equip six active and two reserve squadrons (presently three and one). Those squadrons will be composed of both Cobras and a second type, most likely the AH-64.

The development and widespread deployment of Soviet Mil-24 'Hind' gunships from the early 1970s brought about an entirely new threat scenario for US attack helicopters. It became increasing obvious that helicopters hitherto confined solely to ground attack might one day have to face adversaries with similar capabilities over the same battlefield. In order to carry out their mission of troop carrier escort and anti-armour attack, US 'attack' helicopters could therefore be well served by having their own air-to-air capability to clear any opposing heliborne forces.

Bell consequently undertook to marry the well proven AIM-9 Sidewinder AAM to the SeaCobra under a Naval Aviation Systems Command evaluation programme. In order to give its attack helicopter force the widest possible AAM capability, the Marines have asked for compatibility of the AIM-9L with both the AH-1J and T. Various installations have been proposed by Bell and test firings are being conducted for the first service installations in 1984.

In order to retain a dual anti-air/ground attack capability for both SeaCobra variants, Bell has tested the AIM--9L from launch points above and below the stub wingtips. Although either of these launcher stations are more desirable than utilising existing weapons hardpoints, it is now apparent that it will initially be easier to carry Sidewinders on the Nos 1 and 4 stations of the AH-1J and these installations will probably be fitted to Marine aircraft during 1984, work having been carried out on associated wiring and a new control box. A further series of modifications will be necessary to position Sidewinder launchers on the wingtips of the AH-1T. Bell has proposed a maximum of four AIM-9Ls for the AH-1T, two on new upper wingtip pylons and two on the lower outboard station.

A further milestone in the evolution of the Cobra was achieved on 16 November 1983 with the first flight of the Development Test AH-1T Plus SuperCobra from Bell's Arlington, Texas research centre. Resplendent in a dark blue paint scheme with gold cobras running the full length of each fuselage side BuAer No 161022 was powered by twin General Electric T700-401 engines which were developed and qualified by the Navy for the SH-60 LAMPS helicopter. Rated at 1,625shp each, these engines give a 65% increase in installed power compared with the twin-pack engine used on the standard AH-1T. Approval for up to 44 SuperCobras was given in May 1984, with first deliveries to the Marines scheduled for 1986.

13.
Tank Buster

At the end of the Vietnam war the US Army's sizeable attack helicopter force had become an integral part of that service's organic aviation element. In the decade or so following the war, the Army expanded the force still based on one type until the development of the Hughes AH-64 Apache. In the interim period the AH-1G was refined and subjected to a cost-saving rebuild programme that brought the Army new Cobras for old in an extremely short space of time.

The 1970s HueyCobra procurement programme more or less brought the Army back to first base in that the emphasis changed more towards fighting a conventional war over terrain better suited to helicopter operation than was SE Asia. When the UH-1 was conceived, its typical battleground was assumed to be in Europe and today that area still requires a US presence, with increasing note being taken of events in the Middle East. Not that the lessons learned in the hard environment of Vietnam will, hopefully, be forgotten if US forces — or at least, US military equipment — ever become embroiled in combat operations on the South American continent. The US Army has now geared its attack helicopter force to the primary task of disabling enemy armour in the field, that capability being enhanced considerably by a range of sophisticated new weaponry, particularly the Hughes TOW.

Below:
At the end of their sea voyage, US Army Cobras are off-loaded at various European ports. Note how little disassembly is required for shipment.

The origins of the post-Vietnam modernised Cobra programme were laid in the early 1970s when Bell was still in the process of completing AH-1G production, which reached 1,158 machines by 1972, including eight for Spain and the 38 for the Marines. The US Army, consolidating the airborne assets it had acquired and proved in combat, turned its attention to the dormant AAFSS competition which the AH-1G had in effect bypassed. By mid-1971 the programme was still very much alive, the contending aircraft — Sikorsky's S-66 and Lockheed's AH-56, continuing flight testing while their rival from Texas re-entered the arena, albeit on a purely experimental basis. Although not primarily intended for the AAFFS competition, Bell built single and twin-engined examples of the Model 309 KingCobra, two design studies which linked the Army AH-1G and the Marines' AH-1J/T. Both machines had the 'stretched' 49ft fuselage and 48ft diameter rotor. The first aircraft (N309J) had an 1,800shp UACL T400-CP-400 Turbo Twin Pac engine and made its maiden flight on 10 September 1971.

Featuring a 'wedge' shaped ventral fin similar to that of the first example, the second KingCobra made its maiden flight in January 1972 powered by a Lycoming T55-L-7C turboshaft of 2,050shp. Wing span was increased to 13ft to permit greater fuel load and external stores carrying capability and although initially flying with the short nose of the AH-1G, the contours were curved and later elongated to accommodate a FLIR (Forward Looking Infra-Red) sensor.

Above:
The only European nation to order Cobras so far has been Spain, which now has four from its delivery of eight. They equip *Esc 007* **in the naval anti-shipping role.** *Bell*

Below:
The two KingCobras get airborne. The Army single-engined version is in the foreground, with the Marines' twin behind. *Bell*

Military equipment fit extended to a laser rangefinder, low light-level television, TSU, HUD and INS, and an enlarged nose turret ammunition bay. The turret gun was either a 20mm or 30mm weapon and a wide range of stores could be carried on four hardpoints under 13ft span wings, including eight TOW missiles and two 2.75in FFAR pods.

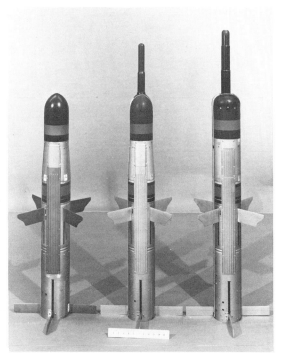

Above:
TOW family. One of the most successful anti-tank missiles of all time, the Hughes BGM-71 series has become the primary helicopter missile weapon of the 1980s. At left is the basic model, Improved TOW is in the centre and the more advanced TOW 2 is on the right. *Hughes*

Below:
The Model 249 was the YAH-1S Modernised Cobra (61-6019) fitted experimentally with a four-bladed rotor developed for the Model 412. *Bell*

The KingCobra was formally presented to the US military on 23 September 1971 and was entered in the fly-off with the Cheyenne and Blackhawk the following year. Both KingCobras grossed 14,000lb, 1,000lb less than the AH-1T and 2,000lb more than AH-1S.

Flight tests of the two KingCobras gave Bell valuable data on which to base development Cobras for the Army and Marines and on 6 March the company was contracted for the first phase of such development for the Army. Under a $24million order, the company embarked on the ICAP — Improved Cobra Armament Programme — to integrate the TOW system into the first eight AH-1Gs. By 28 September 1971 there had been 942 AH-1Gs in Army inventory, and about 71% of these were still active in 1972. The Army accepted its last AH-1G (71-21052) in February 1973.

At the end of January 1974 Bell received a $59.2m US Army contract to modify 101 AH-1Gs to TOW configuration as AH-1Qs. A major proportion of the funding went to Hughes for the missile system and to Sperry Rand's Univac Division for a helmet mounted sighting system. By the end of the year another 189 AH-1Q/TOW helicopters had been ordered, Bell receiving a $54million contract on 16 December.

That some year, a special study group was convened to determine the then-current and future requirements for the Army's HueyCobra force. The group represented Training & Doctrine Command (TRADOC), Army Material Development (DACROM) and Readiness Commands, commodity and field commands and the Cobra project Manager's Office. Under the direction of both US Army Armour and Aviation Centres, the group studied the programme until December 1975. It then made a cost analysis incorporating recommendations from the Department of Army staff and released its findings as Recommended Operational Capability (ROC) data.

Above:
**Instrumentation measuring probe and TOW installation
fitted for AH-1S flight tests with 61-6019.** *Bell*

This data led to a three-phase development programme of the 'definitive' Army Cobra, the AH-1S.

In the interim there were service evaluation aircraft with appropriate designations — YAH-1Q, YAH-1R and YAH-1S. These were respectively eight AH-1Gs developed under ICAP with TOW missile system and helmet sights, one AH-1G modified under the ICAM — improved Cobra Agility and Manoeuvrability — programme with improved transmission, drive train components and the uprated T53-L-703 engine of 1,800shp but no TOW installation, and one YAH-1Q updated to ICAM standard.

Production deliveries of the AH-1Q began on 10 June 1975, and 93 conversions were completed by Bell; 20 were further modified to AH-1S standard and another 63 aircraft based with the US Army in Germany were converted by Dornier using modification kits. These latter were the first of the 'Mod S' Cobras under the three-phase programme which was to last throughout the 1970s. Mod S configuration was found necessary because the full TOW kit required more power to cope with the additional weight. Consequently, the 1,800shp T703 (previously known as the T53-L-703) was installed together with a gearbox and transmission similar to that used on the Marines' AH-1J. The T703 offered 400shp more than the AH-1G/Q powerplant and permitted a 500lb increase in gross weight to 10,000lb total.

The ICAM programme was basically one of structural strengthening and was step two in the modernisation sequence, the resulting aircraft being externally similar to the AH-1G. Step three was to build new AH-1S airframes with considerable external changes, including a distinctive 'flat plate' cockpit canopy. This and other external and internal features were progressively incorporated into earlier Cobras, which were run through steps one and two to produce step three machines. Commonality of equipment finally produced the Upgunned AH-1S, externally similar to production S models but with such features as a Universal gun turret, improved fire control and stores management and some changes in electronic fit.

The US Army formally accepted the initial production AH-1S of 16 March 1977. This and other early machines had the 'long barrel' 20mm gun in the nose turret and the flat plate canopy but lacked an infra-red signature suppressor over the exhaust. A laser rangefinder was built into the 'pinched' nose area above the turret and the aircraft was equipped to carry the full, eight-tube TOW system on strengthened stub wings. Wide chord rotor blades with tapered tips were fitted, these being of all-metal construction. A con-

tinuous cruise speed of 128kts was attainable and
endurance, with 10% fuel reserve, was 2.9hours.
Range with a similar fuel reserve was 280nm.

The latest news is that the Army will not procure
any more AH-1S after 1984, thus ending one chapter
in the Huey story.

Right:
**TOW test firings from an AH-1S earmarked for the
Japanese GSDF.** *Bell*

Below:
**Current toned-down markings on 71-21026, an AH-1S of
the 11th Armoured Cavalry Regt at Fulda, West Germany
seen at Mildenhall UK in May 1983.** *George Pennick*

AH-1S in Combat

Among the nations outside the USA that have had cause to use Bell helicopters in combat, by far the most important is Israel, a country which has not only committed some of the latest Cobras to action but has done so against its intended adversary, armour. Although Bell transport helicopters have been in Israeli service for many years the 1983 Lebanon operation was the first in which the Israeli Air Force was in a position to use Cobra gunships. Reports indicate that they fared well, although not perhaps as well as some sources appear to believe. But in general the investment by a country that does not — indeed cannot — skimp on the quality of its military hardware has proved sound.

Actual operational figures are not disclosed by Irsrael for obvious reasons, but the combat record of the AH-1S was touched on by a senior IAF officer in an October 1982 interview with *Flight International* entitled 'Bekaa Valley Combat'. The IAF deployed in force against Syrian armour in the valley area from 9 June 1982. Relevant parts of the interview were as follows:

Flight International: 'How did your attack helicopters perform?'
IAF: 'We used two types, the Bell AH-1 Cobra and the Hughes 500D Defender. They were used in small numbers and with great caution, mainly because we don't have a lot of experience with such weapons. I can't deny we had quite good success; on the other hand, the survivability of the attack helicopter, mainly

in the environment in which we operated, is low compared with a fighter. That is, unless you plan it very carefully, which we did. We planned each sortie very carefully, that's why our survivability rate was not very high, but acceptable.'
FI: 'So some Cobras and Defenders were shot down?'
IAF: 'One Cobra was shot down, and that's a lot for us.'
FI: 'You preferred the Kfir to helicopters for ground attack?'
IAF: 'Don't draw lessons from this war. If they penetrated the Golan Heights with 4,000 tanks, then the Cobra and Defender would be the best weapon in the first few hours. That's what we bought them for. But in the type of war he had in Lebanon, where we're advancing, the helicopters are operating over 'unclean' ground and the survivability is lower. In that situation the Kfir is more effective. But don't draw the wrong conclusions. The Cobra can be an excellent or a poor weapon, depending on different threats in different areas. We were not disappointed in the Cobra's performance. We knew in advance that it was not the best type of weapon for this area. But we killed tanks and other targets such as Katyusha rocket launchers, APCs, and artillery with the Cobra. So in summary, I can say that the Cobra may be an effective weapon, but its survivability is not.'
FI: 'Why not?'
IAF: 'Because it flies low, is not protected, and every soldier with a Kalashnikov can shoot it down. Very simple.'

Left:
Pilot's instrument panel of AH-1S (70-154941) of B Company, 3rd Battery, US Army at Middle Wallop, July 1979. *R. L. Ward*

Above:
Gunner's position in '941 showing TOW sight. *R. L. Ward*

Right:
Pilot's seat and right side console. *R. L. Ward*

Below:
Flight controls. *R. L. Ward*

Above:
Cockpit showing 'clamshell' canopy open at gunner's station. *R. L. Ward*

Below:
Nose turret with minigun and grenade launcher. *R. L. Ward*

Below:
Quick-release panels for engine access. *R. L. Ward*

Bottom:
Rear view of doghouse and anti-SAM exhaust shield.
R. L. Ward

95

Above:
Port side TOW installation with centre section of tube removed. *R. L. Ward*

Right:
TOW and 21-round 2.75in rocket pod. *R. L. Ward*

Below:
Tailboom with top fairing off and stabiliser airfoil section. *R. L. Ward*

14. World Inventory

More than 50 countries besides the United States have used various versions of Bell and Agusta-built UH-1 derivative models and the following list is a round up of those reported to be in service as of November 1983. Unless specifically qualified the role of all models listed can be assumed to be general 'liaison and utility' (the most common employment for military Hueys). The listing includes some details of base, operating unit and so forth. Countries are grouped into seven broadly geographical areas: Africa, Asia and Australasia, Europe and Scandinavia, Indian Sub-Continent, Middle East, Central and South America, and North America.

Africa

Ethiopia: Operating a mixed force of Soviet and Western-manufactured equipment, the Ethiopian Air Force has six AB204Bs and six UH-1Hs, the latter being flown by Army pilots exclusively in support of ground forces.

Ghana: The Air Force maintains two Bell 212s at Accra for VIP flights.

Guyana: The Defence Force Air Command is a policing force which includes two Bell 212s.

Nigeria: The Police Air Wing operates two Bell 412s.

Somalia: The Aeronautical Corps maintained by this democratic republic has four AB212s, two of which are configured for VIP use.

Tunisia: The Republican Air Force operates 18 AB205s purchased by the Army and six UH-1Hs supplied under US military aid.

Uganda: The Army Air Force has one AB212 and six AB205As and the Police Air Wing has one AB205A.

Zambia: Air Force strength includes a sizeable helicopter force of Western and Soviet types. Among the former are 25 AB205s and two AB212s.

Zimbabwe: There are eight AB205A Cheetahs in use by the Air Force for various duties including medevac. Known examples operated by No 8 Squadron at New Sarum have anti-SAM exhaust shields.

Asia and Australasia

Australia: The Air Force has 13 UH-1Bs for training and 38 UH-1Hs for Army support duties. There are now four Bravo models in RAN inventory, tasked with SAR and liaison duty.

Brunei: The Air Wing of the Royal Brunei Malay Regiment has 11 Bell 212s operating from Berakas Camp on various duties, including training and medevac. One VIP aircraft is used by the Sultan and Government officials.

Burma: The Union of Burma Air Force has 18 UH-1Hs which were supplied by the USA in 1975.

Indonesia: Both the Air Force and the Army air arm operate helicopters, the former having two Bell 204Bs. The Army support force includes 16 Bell 205As and six Bell 212s. All Army aircraft are based at Surabaya, the 205s having been supplied under a US aid agreement.

Japan: All Bell helicopters in inventory are used by the GSDF. There are 83 UH-1B and 75 UH-1H models in service, all of which were built by Fuji. A small proportion of the 54 AH-1S Cobras ordered are in service.

Korea (South): One of the most modern of Asia's air forces, the ROKAF maintains a large helicopter force which includes 15 UH-1Ds and two UH-1Ns for liaison and VIP duties respectively, and two Bell 212s for SAR. The Army has over 200 helicopters including 100 UH-1Ns.

New Zealand: The RNZAF helicopter force is currently based both at home and overseas in Singapore and the Sinai on support duties with its NATO and SEATO allies. In Singapore there is a support unit with three UH-1Hs which operate as part of New Zealand Force South East Asia, and in the Middle East two UH-1Hs loaned from the US support a 29-man RNZAF ground unit operating with the RAAF as part of the Multi-National Observation Force Aviation Support Group in the Sinai. Total RNZAF UH-1 strength is 13 D/H models operating with No 3 Squadron at Hobsville on shared training, liaison and SAR duties. During the Vietnam war some RNZAF Iroquois pilots operated with No 9 Squadron RAAF.

Above:
This Royal New Zealand Air Force Iroquois is NZ3805 of No 3 Squadron, seen c1979.

Singapore: The Republican Air Force has a single helicopter unit operating an all-Bell fleet, this being No 120 (Condor) Squadron at Tengah. Current inventory is 17 UH-1Bs, 30 UH-1Hs and two Bell 212s.

Taiwan: The Chinese Nationalist Army has 50 UH-1Hs, all of which were assembled by AIDC at Taichung.

Thailand: The Thai Air Force, Navy and Army all have a large inventory of UH-1 variants and others are operated by the Border Police. The Air Force has 60 UH-1Hs and 10 212s, and four SAR UH-1Hs are maintained by the Navy. The Army has 90 UH-1B/Ds and the police air component has 10 204Bs, 11 205s and two 205As for general duties. Air Force H models are operated by No 63 Squadron of the 6th Wing along with other types.

Vietnam: Since the North conquered the South in 1975, the Vietnamese People's Air Force has maintained a percentage of the US aircraft captured, including a small number of ex-SVNAF UH-1Hs.

Europe and Scandinavia

Austria: The Air Force has 25 AB212s shared between Helicopter Wing No 1 at Tulln-Langenlebarn and No 3 at Linz-Horsching.
West Germany: The Air Force has 120 UH-1D models and the Army 195.
Greece: The Air Force has 22 AB205s and two Bell 212s for VIP duties; the Navy has five ASW AB212s and the Army 50-plus UH-1Hs and AB205s.
Italy: now phasing out its elderly AB204s, the Air Force retains 10 for training and three AB212s for SAR. The Army has 40 AB204B models, 100 205A transports and 20 AB412s. The Navy has 54 AB212 ASW models.
Norway: The Air Force has 25 UH-1Bs.
Spain: The first Spanish UH-1s were six B models for the Army delivered under MAP in 1965 plus two AB204Bs for the Navy. Today seven UH-1Hs serve the Air Force as trainers, with two configured for VIP use. A mixed inventory of 12 AB205 and AB206

Below:
Norwegian Air Force Bell-built UH-1B of *719 Skv* at Bodo, shortly before the 1972 change of the RNAF's code markings to numbers rather than letters. *Mike Hooks*

JetRangers is also maintained. The Navy has four AH-1Gs out of an order for eight ex-US Army machines in 1973 used by *Esc 007*, and 18 AB212s used for ASW work by *Esc 003*. The carrier *Dedalo* normally carries AB212s or Sea Kings to support the Matadors, and AH-1Gs are occasionally embarked.
Sweden: There are seven AB204Bs configured for SAR duties in Air Force inventory and there are 12 AB204Bs employed on Army support duties.
Turkey: The Air Force has 20 UH-1Ds and 12 UH-1Hs for utility duties, four UH-1Hs configured for ECM work and 25 H models on SAR duties. The Army has 20 AB204s and 90 AB205s.
Yugoslavia: The Air Force operates five AB205s and two AB212s.

Middle East

Bahrain: The Police Wing has two Bell 412s.
Iran: Following the Islamic revolution of 1979 Iran cancelled billions of dollars worth of military equipment on order from the USA. The 287 214s and 202 AH-1Js were then based at Isfahan together with 39 214C models, 45 AB205s and five AB212s in use by the Air Force, and the Navy had five AB205s and six 212s. Intelligence reports indicate that the regime of

Ayatollah Khomeini has maintained a proportion of the Shah's aircraft in airworthy condition, spurred on by the need to defend the country against Iraq.

Israel: The Israeli Defence Force/Air Force has 34 Bell 205s and 12 Bell 212s for SAR. There are 30 AH-1Q/S HueyCobras configured for the anti-tank role.

Jordan: The Air Force has 24 AH-1s on order.

Lebanon: The Air Force has 10 AB212s.

Libya: The Air Force has two VIP AB212s.

Morocco: There are 24 AB205s and five AB212s in current inventory.

Oman: The Sultanate of Oman's Air Force has 16 AB205A-1 models, two ex-Royal Flight AB212s for VIP use and SAR duties plus five Bell 214Bs for utility

Below:
Bell UH-1s are no strangers to desert landing grounds. This otherwise barren spot at least has some sea breeze to cool the sweating crew of a Sultan of Oman's Air Force UH-1H.
Bruce Robertson

work. All these helicopters are used by No 3 Squadron at Salalah.

United Arab Emirates: Abu Dhabi has four AB205As and six Bell 205As. Dubai maintains three AB212s and four Bell 214s. North Yemen's Arab Republic Air Force has five AB212s, and one AB212 for VIP flights.

Indian Sub-Continent

Bangladesh; The Defence Force (Air Wing) added US helicopters to inventory between 1977 and 1982, acquiring 11 Bell 212s in the period. The Army has two AB205s.

Pakistan: Although it does not operate any of its own UH-1s, Pakistan had six H models loaned by the US for flood relief in the 1970s. Flown by No 6 Squadron at Dhamial, a unit widely known as the 'disaster and relief squadron' of the PAF, and which operates solely in support of civilian agencies, these aircraft were

suitably decorated with an American flag, albeit incorrectly proportioned and detailed. All were returned to the USA and during 1971-72 were on the strength of the 182nd Avn Co at Fort Bragg, NC.

Central and South America and Caribbean

Argentina: From almost total obscurity as far as the general public in Europe was concerned, the Argentinian armed forces came under almost microscopic scrutiny during the 1982 Falklands war with Britain and were quickly the focus of attention of the news media of the world. What publicity there was at the time dealt only briefly with Argentinian helicopter operations in the Falklands and the 'man in the street' was told little of the part played by Bell helicopters 'on the other side'. Indeed, the first glimpse of any military UH-1 for many people in the UK was when the RNAS Museum at Yeovilton took delivery of a war booty Argentinian Army UH-1H for permanent display. Others were displayed at the Army's Open Day at Middle Wallop in 1982 and recently, one machine, AE-409, has been received on long term loan from the Museum of Army Flying by the Imperial War Museum collection

At the time of the Argentinian invasion of South Georgia on 3 April 1982, both the *Fuerza Aerea Argentina* and the *Comando de Aviacion del Ejercito* (Air Force and Army respectively) had Bell helicopters in inventory. The Air Force had four UH-1Ds coded H-10 to H-13, the total delivered in 1969. There were also two UH-1Hs remaining from three delivered in 1974 and coded H-14 to H-16, and eight Bell 212s, delivered in 1978 and coded H-81 to H-88.

Below:
'Liberated' by British forces at Port Stanley during the 1982 Falklands war, this UH-1H was AE-410 of the Argentine Army. *Soldier Magazine*

Above:
Some Argentine Hueys abandoned on the Falklands were made serviceable, including this H model, ex-AE-410 of the Army. *Barry Wheeler*

Army inventory was 18 out of 20 H models delivered 1971-77, one of which is known to have crashed in 1979. These machines carried codes in the AE-400 range and from published information it is known that these were: AE-400 to AE-407 inclusive, AE-410 to AE-415 inclusive, plus AE-417, AE-418, AE-422 and AE-424. Two 212s delivered in 1976 were also on strength.

Bell helicopters were not employed extensively during the battle for the Falklands, although the Argentinians ferried enough of them to the islands for useful troop transportation and ground support duties. For the record, it is confirmed that a UH-1 was shot down on 20 May and another succumbed to shell fire whilst airborne on 5 June. And on 14 June two Army UH-1s were destroyed near Port Stanley while conducting troop carrier operations. In addition, 'several' UH-1s were claimed destroyed near Goose Green right at the beginning of hostilities, on 1 May.

Eight Army UH-1s (AE-406, AE-409, AE-412, AE-413, AE-417, AE-418, AE-422 and AE-424) were found abandoned in various states of repair at Port Stanley, along with both the Bell 212s, H-83 and H-85. Two machines, AE-409 and AE-422, were ferried to the UK and one of the abandoned machines was refurbished by personnel of No 820 NAS in the Falklands. With some civilian assistance, this H model was put in to flying condition and used by the Falkland Islands Government Air Service (FIGAS). It first flew under 'entirely new management' and registration VP-FBD on 26 August. Resplendent in an all-red paint scheme, this particular Huey was cared for by No 657 Squadron Army Air Corps at Stanley.

In total, the Argentinian Army lost 22 helicopters in the Falklands action, leaving 10 UH-1Hs. The Air Force inventory includes six 212s from the original eight and recent published listings give only four UH-1Ds, leading to the likelihood that the 'several' referred to earlier were in fact Air Force H models. As far as replacements are concerned, helicopters obviously run second to first line combat aircraft, although the Navy is reported to have shown interest in acquiring ASW AB212s to fill a gap created by cancellation of the Westland Lynx intended for seaborne operations from destroyers.

Bolivia: The Air Force has six UH-1Hs for use by the *Grupo Aereo Mixto* (Mixed Air Group) at Colcapirua, delivered in 1975. One of these was written off in August 1977. There are also two Bell 212s in service as VIP transports.

Brazil: Known as H-1 under the Brazilian designation system, the Air Force has 32 UH-1Hs, eight UH-1Ds and five SH-1Ds. One of the D models has been converted to SH-1D standard (presumably to make good the loss of one of six original SH-1Ds lost in September 1980); at least one D model has been armed and some armed H models are known as AH-1Hs. On 30 September 1977 FAB officers carried out the longest helicopter flight on record when they delivered eight UH-1Hs from Fort Worth to Rio, a distance of 5,750 miles. A circuitous route was followed, the aircraft arriving in mid-October. Earlier deliveries of UH-1s from Bell had been by airlift.

Chile: The Air Force has 13 UH-1Hs and the Army three. The Navy operates a small number of UH-1Ds on mixed duties, including SAR.

Colombia: The Air Force has nine UH-1Bs and 12 UH-1Hs.

Dominica: The tiny Republican Air Force has a single helicopter squadron, the inventory of which includes two Bell 205As.

Ecuador: The Air Force has a single Bell 212 for VIP flying and two Bell 214B models. The Army has a single UH-1D in its small helicopter force.

El Salvador: A total of 22 Bell UH-1Hs have been supplied in two batches; at least seven have been lost, six of them in a raid on Ilopango in January 1982 by 'left wing' guerillas, but recent US aid to government forces has undoubtedly made good these losses.

Guatemala: The Air Force has three UH-1Ds, six UH-1Hs, three Bell 212s and six 412s. It was reported in 1982 that Guatemala had rigged all its twin-engined Bell helicopters as gunships/troop carriers for anti-guerilla operations in defiance of a US refusal to supply military UH-1s.

Jamaica: The Defence Force Air Wing has a small helicopter/fixed wing inventory which includes three Bell 212s based at Up Park Camp, Kingston.

Mexico: The Air Force's single helicopter unit includes five Bell 205s and a 212, all of which can be adapted to carry armament in the counter-insurgency role.

Panama: Engaged on liaison, transport and offshore surveillance work rather than having any military role, the Air Force maintains a comparatively large helicopter fleet. Current inventory includes eight UH-1Bs, nine UH-1Hs and four UH-1Ns on VIP duties.

Peru: The Air Force has 16 Bell 212s and nine UH-1Ds; there are six D/H models engaged on Naval utility, plus six AB212s for ASW and surveillance work operating from Italian-built 'Lupo' class frigates.

Philippines: The Air Force has 16 UH-1Hs and 16 412s, the Army 50 UH-1Hs.

Uruguay: The Air Force has five UH-1Bs and four UH-1Hs in the SAR and utility roles respectively.

Venezuela: The Air Force has a mixed force of 20 UH-1D/H models, two UH-1Ns for VIP flights, four 412s and two 214ST models. The Navy maintains 12 AB212s for ASW work and the Army has three UH-1Hs and two Bell 205A models.

North America

Canada: The CAF has 10 CH-118 Iroquois for SAR duties and 52 CH-135 Twin Hueys for SAR and general utility work. Units operating the CH-135s include Air Command's No 427 Squadron at Patawana and No 450 at Ottawa South, the latter unit employing three machines in a VIP Flight. Cold Lake Base Flight also has two for weapons range support and base SAR duties, while No 408 Squadron at CFB Edmonton uses the CH-118 for land forces support.

The US Army inventory includes approximately 4,000 UH-1s, the majority of them H models, although the UH-1C is certainly not extinct. There are about 1,000 AH-1 Cobras, including 490 S models configured for TOW missiles.

The US Marine Corps: Six utility squadrons operate a mix of 126 UH-1E/N models and there are 74 AH-1J SeaCobras and 51 TOW-armed AH-1Ts in three attack squadrons. The Reserve Force has two squadrons of UH-1Es.

The US Air Force has 19 UH-1s in TAC; USAFE has the UH-1N for support duties generally; MAC supports over 120 UH-1Fs, 22 base rescue UH-1Hs and 59 HH-1Ns; and there are four ARRS squadrons with HH-1Hs in the Air Force Reserve.

The US Navy operates TH-1Ls and UH-1Ls for training, and one Reserve Wing has HH-1s in a mixed helicopter inventory.

Bell UH-1H Iroquois

1 FM homing aerials
2 Nose compartment access door
3 Radio and avionics equipment
4 Battery
5 Downward vision window
6 Yaw control rudder pedals
7 Footboards
8 Fire extinguisher
9 Windscreen de-misting air duct
10 Instrument console
11 Instrument panel shroud
12 Windscreen panels
13 Windscreen wipers
14 Starboard jettisonable cockpit door
15 Cockpit eyebrow window
16 Handgrip

17 VHF aerial
18 Cockpit fresh air intakes
19 Overhead systems switch panel
20 Pitot head
21 Pilot's seat (armoured type)
22 Cyclic pitch control column handgrip
23 Safety harness

24 Centre instrument panel
25 Control column
26 Cockpit door jettison mechanism
27 Seat mounting rail
28 Collective pitch control lever
29 Cockpit step
30 Port lower navigation light
31 Door latch
32 Co-pilot's seat (conventional type)

33 Sliding side window panel
34 First aid kits
35 Cabin roof frame construction
36 Cabin skin panelling
37 DF loop aerial
38 Litter installation (maximum six stretchers)
39 Stretcher mounting post
40 Forward, hinged, cabin door, port and starboard
41 Cabin side pillar construction
42 Winch mounting pad (four alternative positions)
43 Heater distribution ducting

44 Forward external stores pylon mounting lugs
45 Landing skid front strut
46 Winch motor
47 Rescue hoist/winch

48 Heating air distribution ducting
49 Cabin floor panelling
50 Floor beam construction
51 Underfloor fuel tank; total fuel capacity 220 US gal (833 litres)
52 Underfloor control linkages
53 External load-slinging cargo hook
54 Cargo hook stabilising spring
55 Medical attendant's folding seat

56 Port upper navigation lights
57 Ventilating air intake
58 Detachable rotor-head front fairing
59 Generator
60 Ventilating air intake
61 Starboard upper navigation lights
62 Two-bladed main rotor
63 Laminated blade-root stiffeners
64 Blade root attachment joints
65 Semi-rigid rotor head mechanism

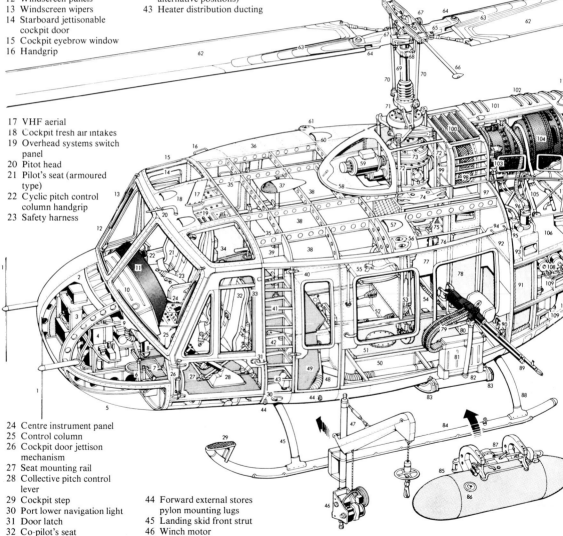

104

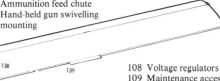

66 Rotor stabilising beam
67 Blade counterbalance weights
68 Pitch angle control rods
69 Main rotor mast
70 Rotor head control rods
71 Swash plate mechanism
72 Swash plate control rods
73 Main rotor gearbox
74 Gearbox mounting sub-frame

75 Gearbox support structure
76 Control rod hydraulic actuator
77 Rearward sliding main cabin door panel, port and starboard
78 Centre section fuel tank
79 Ammunition feed chute
80 Hand-held gun swivelling mounting

104 Avco-Lycoming T53-L-13 turboshaft engine
105 Engine bearer struts
106 Fireproof engine mounting deck
107 Sliding cabin door rail

108 Voltage regulators
109 Maintenance access steps
110 Electrical equipment bays
111 0.50in (12.7mm) machine gun
112 Cartridge case collector bag

81 Ammunition box
82 Gun pintle mounting
83 Pylon mounting struts
84 Port landing skid
85 External fuel tank, capacity 60 US gal (227 litres)
86 Fuel filler cap
87 Tank mounting adaptor
88 Landing skid rear strut
89 0.30in (7.62mm) machine gun (carried with cabin door removed)
90 Heater distribution ducts
91 Fuselage flank fuel tanks, port and starboard
92 Cabin rear bulkhead
93 Maintenance access step
94 Handgrip
95 Fuel system filter
96 Bleed air control valve
97 Engine bay forward fireproof bulkhead
98 Engine intake guard
99 Engine/gearbox shaft coupling
100 Filtered air intake
101 Detachable engine cowling panels
102 Cooling air scoops
103 Engine accessory equipment

113 Ammunition box
114 Ground power socket
115 Static inverters
116 Centrally mounted oil cooler
117 Engine bay rear fireproof bulkhead
118 Tail rotor shaft coupling
119 UHF aerial
120 Anti-collision light
121 Exhaust pipe
122 Smoke generator
123 Engine exhaust nozzle
124 Tail rotor control cable linkage
125 Tailcone attachment joint frame
126 Tailcone extension section
127 Longeron bolted joints
128 Tailcone lower longeron
129 Frame and stringer construction
130 All-moving tailplane control linkage
131 Upper longeron
132 Tail rotor transmission shaft
133 Shaft bearings
134 Dorsal spine shaft housing

135 Main rotor blade honeycomb core construction
136 Extruded aluminium D-section blade spar
137 Leading edge anti-erosion sheathing (stainless steel)
138 Laminated glass-fibre blade skins
139 Fixed tab
140 Starboard all-moving tailplane
141 Tailplane torque shaft
142 Port all-moving tailplane construction
143 Radio compass transmitter
144 VHF navigation aerial
145 Control access panel
146 Sloping tail pylon spar joint frame
147 Bevel drive gearbox
148 Tail rotor control cables
149 Tail rotor drive shaft
150 Tail pylon construction
151 Final drive right-angle gearbox
152 FM communications aerial
153 Two-bladed tail rotor
154 Blade root attachments
155 Tail rotor blade pitch control mechanism
156 Honeycomb core blade construction
157 Laminated glass-fibre blade skins
158 Tail navigation light
159 Tail rotor protecting tailskid

Appendices

Fuselage length: 39ft 7½in (12.08m)
Height overall: 14ft 7in (4.45m)
Empty weight: 4,502lb (2,042kg)
Max take-off weight: 8,500lb (3,856kg)
Max speed at AUW of 6,000lb (2,994kg): 138mph (222km/hr)
Economic cruise speed: 126mph (203km/hr)
Rate of climb at sea level: 2,350ft (715m)/min
Hovering ceiling in ground effect (IGE): 8,200ft (2,500m)
Hovering ceiling out of ground effect (OGE): 12,500ft (3,810m)
Range: 253 miles (407km) with 800lb (363kg) payload and 10% reserve

UH-1H

Type: Single-rotor general purpose helicopter
Engine: One 1,400shp Lycoming T53-L-13 turboshaft
Fuel capacity: 220 US gal (832 litres)
Accommodation: Crew of two and up to 14 troops or six litters and a medical attendant or 3,880lb (1,759kg) of freight
Main rotor diameter: 48ft (14.63m)
Tail rotor diameter: 8ft 6in (2.59m)
Fuselage length: 41ft 10¾in (12.77m)
Height overall: 14ft 6in (4.42m)
Empty weight: 4,937lb (2,255kg)
Max take-off weight: 9,500lb (4,309kg)

1   Specification

UH-1B

Type: Single-rotor utility helicopter
Engine: One 960shp Lycoming T53-L-5 or 1,100shp T53-L-9 or T53-L-11 shaft-turbine
Fuel capacity: 165 US gal (625 litres)
Accommodation: Crew of two plus seven troops or three litters and medical attendant
Main rotor diameter: 44ft (13.4m)
Tail rotor diameter: 8ft 6in (2.59m)

Below:
UH-1H. *Pilot Press*

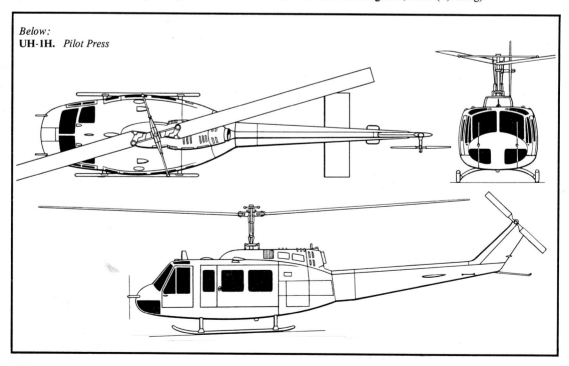

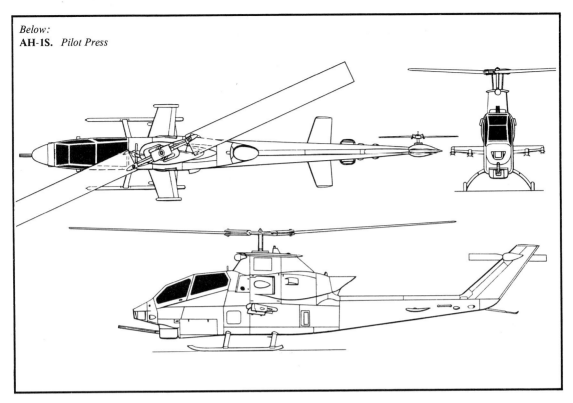

Below:
AH-1S. *Pilot Press*

Max level speed: 127mph (204km/hr)
Max permissible diving speed: 127mph (204km/hr)
Max cruising speed: 127mph (204km/hr)
Economic cruising speed: 127mph (204km/hr) at 5,700ft (1,735m)
Hovering ceiling IGE: 13,600ft (4,145m)
Hovering ceiling OGE: 1,100ft (335m)
Range: 318 miles (511km) at sea level with 9,500lb (4,309kg), max fuel and no reserves

AH-1G

Type: Single-rotor attack helicopter
Engine: One 1,400shp Lycoming T53-L-13 turboshaft
Fuel capacity: 247 US gal (1,345 litres)
Accommodation: Pilot and gunner in tandem seating
Main rotor diameter: 44ft (13.41m)
Tail rotor diameter: 8ft 6in (2.59m)
Fuselage length: 44ft 5in (13.54m)
Height overall: 13ft 5½in (4.10m)
Operating weight: 6,096lb (2,765kg)
Max take-off weight: 9,500lb (4,309kg)
Max diving speed: 219mph (352km/hr)
Cruising speed: 166mph (267km/hr)
Rate of climb at sea level: 1,680ft (512m)/min
Hovering ceiling IGE: 10,800ft (3,290m)
Range: 362 miles (582km) with 9,254lb (4,197kg)

2   Military Designations, Model Numbers and Derivatives

Model 204
XH-40
YH-40
XH-1A
HU-1
UH-1A
TH-1A
RH-2

Model 533
AB 204
AB 204B
Fuji 204B-2
YUH-1B
UH-1B
NUH-1B
UH-1C
UH-1M
HueyTug

Model 205
YUH-1D
UH-1D
AB 205
AB 205A-1
JUH-1D
UH-1E
TH-1E
HH-1K
TH-1L
UH-1L
XH-48A
UH-1F
UH-1P
UH-1H
CUH-1H
HH-1H
EH-1H
UH-1V

Model 208 Twin Delta

Model 212
UH-1N
VH-1N

Model 212 ASW

Model 214 Huey-Plus

Model 214A

Model 214B BigLifter

Model 214C

Model 214ST

Model 412

Model 209
AH-1G
JAH-1G
TH-1G
AH-1R

Model 309 KingCobra
AH-1J
AH-1Q

Model 249
AH-1S
AH-1T

3   Serial Numbers

UH-1A-BF:

57-6095/6103	(9)
58-2078/2093	(16)
58-3017/3047	(31)
59-1607/1716	(110)
60-3530/3535	(16)

Total includes one XH-1A for armament trials and 14 UH-1As with dual controls and blind flying instrumentation.

YUH-1B-BF:

60-3546/3549	(4)

UH-1B-BF:

60-3550/3619	(70)
61-686/803	(118)
62-1872/2105	(234)
62-4566/4605	(40)
62-12515/12549	(35)
62-12550/12555	(6)
63-8500/8658	(159)
63-8659/8738	(80)
63-12903/12952	(50)
64-13902/14100	(199)

UH-1C-BF:

64-14101/14191	(91)
65-9416/9564	(149)
65-12738/12744	(7)
65-12853/12856	(4)
66-491/745	(255)
66-15000/15245	(246)
66-15358/15360	(3)

YUH-1D:

60-6028/6034	(7)

UH-1D-BF:

62-2106/2113	(8)
62-12351/12372	(22)
63-12956/13002	(47)
64-13492/13585	(94)
64-13594/13901	(308)
65-9565/10135	(571)
65-12773/12776	(4)
65-12847/12852	(6)
65-12857/12895	(39)
66-746/1210	(465)
66-8574/8577	(4)
66-16000/16305	(307)

UH-1E:

BuAer 15266/151299	(34)
151840/151877	(48)
152416/152439	(24)
153740/153767	(28)
154750/154780	(31)
154943/154969	(27)
155337/155367	(31)

TH-1E:

154730/154749	(20)

UH-1F-BF:

63-13141/13145	(5)
63-13147/13148	(2)
63-13151/13155	(5)
63-13157/13159	(3)
63-13163/13164	(2)
64-15477/15485	(9)
64-15487/15492	(6)
64-15494/15501	(8)
65-7911/7925	(16)
65-7927/7928	(2)
65-7930/7935	(6)
65-7937/7965	(29)
66-1211/1218	(8)
66-1220/1227	(8)
66-1229/1240	(12)
66-1242/1244	(3)
66-1246/1248	(3)
66-1250	(1)

UH-1P:

63-13146	(1)
63-13149/13150	(2)
63-13156	(1)
63-13160/13162	(3)
63-13165	(1)
64-15476	(1)
64-15486	(1)
64-15493	(1)
65-7926	(1)
65-7929	(1)
65-7936	(1)
66-1219	(1)
66-1228	(1)
66-1239	(1)
66-1241	(1)
66-1245	(1)
66-1249	(1)

TH-1F:

66-1225/1250	(26)

AH-1G-BF:

64-7015/7016	(2)
66-15246/15357	(112)
67-15450/15869	(420)
68-15000/15213	(214)
68-17020/17113	(94)
69-16410/16447	(38)
70-15936/16105	(170)
71-20983/21052	(70)

BuAer Nos 157204/157241 were allocated to the USMC's first 38 AH-1Gs but not used, although 67-15850 did become BuAer 57204 at least on paper. The following AH-1Gs were operated by the Marines: 68-15037, 038, 039, 045, 046, 072, 073, 079, 080, 085; 15104, 105, 112, 113, 134, 140, 165, 170, 190, 194, 198; 15213; 15213; 68-17023, 027, 041, 045, 049, 062, 066, 070, 082, 086, 090; 17101, 105, 108.

TAH-1G:
A number of AH-1Gs used for training.

JAH-1G-BF:
71-20985 (used for testing).

UH-1H-BF:

66-16307/17144	(838)
67-17145/17859	(715)
67-18411/18413	(3)
67-18558/18577	(20)
67-19475/19537	(63)
68-15214/15778	(565)
68-15779/15794	(16)
68-16050/16628	(579)
69-15000/15959	(960)
69-16650/16670	(21)
69-16692/16732	(41)
70-15700/15874	(175)
70-15913/15932	(20)
70-16200/16518	(319)
71-20000/20339	(340)
72-21465/21649	(185)
73-21661/21860	(200)
73-22072/22135	(64)
74-22295/22544	(250)
76-22650/22672	(23)

CUH-1H: Initial designation for Canadian UH-1H which became CH-118 under CAF system; conversions to EH-1H electronic warfare version.

HH-1H-BF:

70-2457/2485	(29)

AH-1J:

BuAer 157757/157805	(49)
159210/159229	(20)
160105/160119	(15)

HH-1K:
BuAer 157177/157203   (27)

TH-1L:
BuAer 157806/157850   (45)

UH-1L:
BuAer 157851/157858   (45)

UH-1M:
Conversions from UH-1C

UH-1N-BF:
68-10778	(1)
69-6600	(1)
69-6603/6636	(34)
69-6638/6654	(17)
69-6659/6666	(8)
69-6670	(1)
69-7536/7537	(2)
BuAer 158230/158259	(30)
158260/158291	(32)
158548/158550	(3)
158552/158553	(2)
158555	(1)
158558/158562	(5)
158762/158785	(24)
159186/159209	(24)
159565	(1)
159774/159777	(4)
160165/160177	(13)
160438/160461	(24)
160619/160624	(6)
160827/160837	(11)

HH-1N:
68-10773	(1)
68-10774/10776	(3)
69-6601/6602	(2)
70-2457/2485	(29)

VH-1N:
69-6637	(1)
69-6655/6658	(4)
69-6667/6669	(3)
69-7538	(1)
BuAer 158277/8278	(2)
158551	(1)
158554	(1)
158556/8557	(2)

CUH-1N:
50 aircraft to CAF as CH-135
with serials 135101/135150.

AH-1Q-BF:
92 conversions from AH-1G.

AH-1R:
AH-1G conversion.

AH-1S-BF:
Conversions plus production:
76-22567/22626	(60)
76-22691/22698	(8)
77-22729/22811	(83)
78-23042/23125	(84)
79-23185/23252	(185)
80-23509/23540	(32)

AH-1T:
BuAer 160107/160109	(3)
160742/160748	(8)
160797/160826	(29)
161015/161022	

161022 was the first AH-1T Plus SuperCobra.
Subsequent contracts being met through 1984.

4   Record Flights

In July 1960, the HU-1 claimed for the USA six world helicopter class records under Federation Aeronautique Internationale rules. The FAI confirms and registers world records for all types of aircraft and metric measurement is used by international agreement. Helicopter records are certified in the name and nationality of the pilot in command irrespective of the number of persons in the crew. A record is deemed to be new only if it exceeds that of the previous holder by not less than 1%. In addition, new ones are recognised. The first series of UH-1 record flights were made by Army pilots Maj G. J. Boyle III, Col Jack Marinelli and Chief Warrant Officer C. V. Turvey.

19 July 1960: Time to climb to 3,000 metres (9,843ft) — 3 minutes 29.1 seconds (Boyle); record previously held by France.
Time to climb to 6,000m (19,686ft) — 8 minutes 7.1 seconds (Boyle); record previously held by France.

22 July 1960: 3km (1 mile) speed run, restricted altitude — 254.286km/hr (158.040mph) (Turvey); no previous record.*

23 July 1960: 500km (310 miles) speed run over closed circuit — 238.906km/hr (148.481mph) (Marinelli); record previously held by USSR.
50km (31 miles) speed over closed circuit — 238.906km/hr (148.481mph) (Marinelli); record previously held by USSR.

26 July 1960: 100km (62.14 miles) speed run over closed circuit: 228.831km/hr (142.220mph) (Turvey); record previously held by USSR.

In 1962, the YUH-1D claimed a second series of records. Again three Army pilots flew the aircraft — Capt Boyce B. Buckner, Lt-Col Leland Wilhelm and Capt W. F. Gurley:

13 April 1962: Climb to given altitude: 5 minutes 47.4 seconds to 6,000m (Buckner); record previously held by USA.

14 April 1962: Time to climb to given altitude: 2 minutes 17.3 seconds to 3,000m (Wilhelm); record previously held by USA.

20 April 1962: Speed in 1,000km closed circuit: 217km/hr (134.9mph) (Gurley).

In September and October 1964 another assault was made on the record books by a UH-1D. The flights were made from Fort Worth and the US Army Aviation Test Activity centre at Edwards AFB. Five pilots were involved, all from USAATA; Capt Michael N. Antoniou, Maj John A. Johnston; CWO Joseph C. Watts, CWO Emery B. Nelson and Capt William L. Welter Jr.

16 September 1964: 1,000km speed in closed circuit — 140km/hr (87mph) (Johnston); record previously held by USA (UH-1D, 20 April 1962).*

18 September 1964: Distance over closed circuit — 2,600.189km (1,614.6 miles) (Johnston); record previously held by USSR.

23 September 1964: 2,000km speed run in closed circuit — 215.626km/h (133.9mph) (Watts); record previously held by USSR.

27 September 1964: Distance in straight line — 2,170.7km (1,348.8 miles) (Antoniou).
Closed circuit distance — 1,999km (1,242.8 miles) (Watts); no previous record.

27 September 1964: Distance in a straight line — 2,170km (1,348.8) miles (Edwards AFB to Rogers, Arkansas) (Antoniou); record previously held by USA.

7 October 1964: Time to climb to 3,000m — 2 minutes 9.6 seconds (Nelson).
Time to climb to 6,000m — 4 minutes 35.8 seconds (Nelson), record previously held by USA (YHU-1D, 13 April 1962),
Time to climb to 9,000m (29, 529ft) — 9 minutes 13.7 seconds (Welter); record previously held by USA.

From 16 November to 14 December 1964 the UH-1D flew a further series of records, all but one at Edwards. The last of 11 records was made at Edwards, one being under the jurisdiction of the US Army Aviation Test Board at Fort Rucker, commanded by Lt-Col Richard J. Kennedy. Kennedy himself flew one and there were seven USAATA pilots: Capt D. P. Wray, Maj L. R. Dennis, Maj J. K. Foster, Capt R. A. Chubboy, Maj B. L. Odneal, Maj E. F. Sampson and Capt J. F. Cromer

16 November 1964: 3km speed — 278km/hr (173.19mph) (Wray); no previous record.

20 November 1964: 15/25km (9-15 miles) speed — 276km/hr (171.65mph) (Wray); no previous record.
15/25km speed — 278km/hr (172.9mph) (Dennis); no previous record.*
100km speed — 264kmr (164.12mph) (Foster); no previous record.*

21 November 1964: Speed over 100km (62.14 miles) — 270km/hr (168.12mph) (Foster); record previously held by USSR.

23 November 1964: 500km speed — 274km/hr (170.75mph) (Chubboy); no previous record.*
500km speed — 283km/hr (176.8mph) (Odneal); record previously held by USA (UH-1).*

25 November 1964: 1,000km speed — 289km/hr (180.14mph) (Cromer); record previously held by USA (UH-1).*

11 December 1964: Altitude without payload: 10,713m (35,150ft) (Sampson); record previously held by USA.*

14 December 1964: Altitude without payload: 7,747m (25,418ft) (Kennedy); no previous record.*

Weight adjustments were made to the UH-1D in order to qualify it for the various record attempts, and on nine of the flights it was fitted with the 540 rotor. The result was that the US claimed 35 of the 61 world helicopter records recognised at that time, way head of its nearest rival, Russia, which held 17. The UH-1D gave Bell 27 of these US world records, or 77.2%. All flights were co-ordinated by Bell engineer R. S. Stansbury and Maj Odneal, Chief VTOL Division and service test pilot of USAATA, and observed by officials of the National Aeronautic Association, the US representative group of the FAI — but despite this the FAI in Paris has not officially ratified those records marked with an asterix.*

Above:
The well-known 'Heer' titlings adorn German Army Hueys — this one being photographed at Kiel in August 1975. Note the double wheel attachments.
R. Lindsay via R. L. Ward

Below:
The AB204 AS gave the Italian Navy a fast, potent anti-shipping helicopter from 1965. *Mike Hooks*

Left:
Early production Fuji-Bell 204B with civil registration JA-9009.
Barry Wheeler